HOW TO SUCCEED IN

Activity Based Selling

HOW TO SUCCEED IN

Activity
Creating the Self-Motivation

Based
Needed for

Selling
Peak Sales Performance

RUSSELL MERCK

Gold Star Publishing
North Haven, CT

Permissions:

The "Beach Scene" is reprinted with the permission of Simon & Schuster, from *Creative Imagery* by William Fezler. Copyright © 1989 by Dr. William Fezler.

Repetitive reading example on page 163 is from *The Greatest Salesman in the World* by Og Mandino. Copyright © 1967 by Og Mandino. Used by permission of Bantam Books, a division of Bantam Doubleday Dell Publishing Group, Inc.

Cover Design:

Cover design by Pat Shoemaker of Shoemaker Design, 87 Willow Street, New Haven, CT (203) 562-4030.

Copyright © 1997 by Russell Merck. All rights reserved. No part of this work may be reproduced in any form, or by any means, without the permission of the publisher. Exceptions are made for brief excerpts to be used in published reviews.

ISBN: 0-9652524-0-X

Library of Congress Catalog Card Number 96-76375

Printed in the United States of America

Attention Corporations, Career Agencies, Professional Organizations, and Trade Associations: Quantity discounts are available on bulk purchases of this book for educational purposes, fund raising, or gift giving. Companion audio and video learning aids are also available by special request. For more information, please contact Gold Star Publishing, P.O. Box 762, North Haven, CT 06473. (800) 775-9834.

This book is dedicated to anyone who has ever had to identify prospects, make cold calls, or do paperwork when they really didn't feel like doing it.

"There is quality in quantity."

-- Branch Ricky

"A salesperson's daily grind is a continuous long-term process, one that is taken in methodical daily steps. It is the daily work they must do to generate sales."

-- Ken West

Acknowledgments

It has taken more than two years to research, write, edit, and finalize this book. Over that period of time, a number of people have played an integral part in making this book a reality. These individuals are deserving of, and have, my deepest gratitude. I would like to acknowledge the following people for their contribution to this work:

My first thanks goes to my editor, Bob Binnie. Bob generously and selflessly volunteered to edit this book at no charge. His frank and honest comments helped significantly in shaping the style and content of the book. I will be forever grateful for the substantial amount of effort he put into this project.

I also wish to thank those who reviewed early drafts of chapters and gave me much needed encouragement. That list includes, but is not limited to: Jeff Konspore, Jim Cathcart, Sheila Murray Bethel, and my parents, Dean and Nelda Merck.

Special thanks to those who took on the tedious task of proofreading the final manuscript: Jan and Cathy Ozolins, Peter Krembs, Carla Fischer, Lori Brantner, Nanette Minor, Randy Tyler, Ron Rael, J.O. Dravis, Charlie Miller, Ian See, and Maureen Labrum.

Thanks to Pat Shoemaker, the talented graphic artist who turned a sketchy idea for a cover design into the work of art you hold in your hands.

Thanks most of all to my dear wife Hayes. She not only helped with the proofreading, but believed in me, encouraged me, understood when I spent time on the book instead of with her, and in general *allowed* me to take on and complete this project.

Last but certainly not least, I want to thank God, without whom none of this would have been possible. Many days it was only my faith in Him and my belief that He wanted me to write this book that kept me going. Should any honor or accolades come from writing this book, all the credit goes to Him.

TABLE OF CONTENTS

Introduction
What is Activity-Based Selling?   1

The "Results Equation" • What is "Activity-Based Selling?" • The Unique Challenge of Activity-Based Selling • Rising to the Challenge • A Word About "Motivation" • About This Book • Not so Sexy

Part I: Understanding Activity

Chapter 1
The Shortest (and Most Important) Chapter in this Book   11

A Compelling "Why" • Inner Peace • The Need for Honesty

Chapter 2
It's Not All Discipline   15

In the Marine Corps • Our Thoughts Govern Our Activity • Getting Past the Walls • A Word of Warning • Why is Activity Easier for Some?

Chapter 3
Enabling Beliefs   23

Beliefs as Mental Software • Activity Level is a Critical Ingredient for Sales Success • Consistency Makes Activity Easier and More Effective • Success and Failure Occur in Small Steps Over Time • Work is a Potential Source of Pleasure • I Can Succeed and I Will Succeed • Eliminating Limiting Beliefs • Integrating Enabling Beliefs

Chapter 4
Defining Key Activities and Target Levels   34

Defining Your Sales Process • Three Classes of Sales Activities • Discretionary Activities • Non-Discretionary Activities •

Semi-Discretionary Activities • Process Goals vs. Results Goals • Amount • Length of Time • Time Limit • What is the Appropriate Level of Key Sales Activities? • Time Frame: When to Reset Process Goals • Congratulations • Application Exercises

Part II: Creating Activity

Introduction to Part II   47

Chapter 5
Health and Vitality   49
The Importance of Vitality to Sales Activity • Energy Drains • Sleep Deprivation • Depression • Energy Draining Dietary Habits • Circadian Rhythms • Additional Energy Drains • Energy Boosters • Aerobic Exercise • The Sugar Blues • Relaxation • Caffeine • Power Breathing • Q&A • Application Exercises

Chapter 6
Mental Imaging   79
The Magical Power of Visualization • Why the Emphasis on Behavior? • The Five Senses: Building Blocks of Powerful Mental Images • Creating Sales Activity • Q&A • Application Exercises

Chapter 7
Managing Negative Emotions   93
Emotions, What are They? • What Causes Emotions? • Conditioned Responses • Emotions Created by Meaning • Physical State • Identifying Your Debilitating Emotions • Techniques for Managing Emotions • Before You Try Any Technique ... • Manage the Meaning • Change Your Body • Manage Your Environment • Get Some Perspective • Implementing the Techniques • Q&A • Application Exercises

Chapter 8
Tracking 117
Shaping Behavior Through Positive Reinforcement • Tracking as a Means of Positive Reinforcement • How to Use Tracking as a Motivational Tool • The Phone Log • Other Activity Logs • The Time Log • Other Performance Indicators • Graphical Display of Data • Q&A • Application Exercises

Chapter 9
Discipline 137
Discipline, What is It? • Used Sparingly, Discipline is a Great Motivational Tool • Developing Discipline • Learn to Recognize Discipline Opportunities • Exercise the Discipline Muscle • Explore the Feeling • Beware Overuse • Q&A • Application Exercises

Chapter 10
Miscellaneous Motivational Techniques 155
Miscellaneous Tools • Managing Internal Dialogue • Turning Work into "Flow" • Motivation Through Repetitive Reading • Visual Reminders • Using a Conditioning Book • Using Public Commitment as a Motivational Tool

Part III: Refining Activity

Chapter 11
Assessing the Impact of Your Activity 175
We Want Activity that Produces Results • Change Nothing • Increase Activity Levels • Effectiveness Ratios • Target Markets • Change Your Sales Strategy • Activity is Not Enough

Conclusion: Back to Why 193

Index 201

About the Author 205

HOW TO SUCCEED IN

Activity Based Selling

Introduction
What is Activity-Based Selling?

"'Activity-Based Selling' is a specific type of sales where success is highly dependent on the number of prospects one contacts."

-- Russell Merck

This book is about sales activity: generating leads, making phone calls, and seeing prospects. When most salespeople think of becoming more effective, they think of improving their persuasion skills, or learning more about their products, or perhaps earning some professional designation. Rarely does anyone consider training themselves to systematically increase their level of activity. Most salespeople would agree that the number of leads they generate, calls they make, and people they see has a huge impact on their bottom-line. Yet very few spend any time at all training themselves to increase the level of these activities.

I believe there are two reasons for this. First, most people don't consciously focus on the *value* of their activity. When asked they will tell you they think activity level is extremely important, but if left alone seldom would it enter their mind. Second, salespeople don't know *how* to train themselves to increase their activity. There aren't any seminars, books, or tapes that focus specifically on increasing activity. This book will help to fill that gap.

The Results Equation

Few would argue that in sales, results are a combination of two factors: activity level and the effectiveness of that activity. The results equation looks like this:

$$Results = Activity \times Effectiveness$$

If we define *Activity* as the number of prospects we see and *Effectiveness* as the percentage of prospects we successfully close, then *Results* represents the number of sales we successfully close or our sales volume.

This book is unique because it focuses exclusively on the activity portion of the equation. It is my firm belief that most of us know what we should do, and it is our inability to get ourselves to consistently do these things that limits our success. One of the fundamental questions of my life is, "How do I get myself to do what I know I should do?" This book documents what I have learned in my attempts to answer that all important question. In the chapters that follow, we will explore together some new methodologies as well as classic techniques from the field of behavior management. And we will consider each specifically as it relates to increasing sales activity. We will explore what causes us to do less than we can and develop strategies for doing all that we can. You will learn to value consistent activity, honestly assess your current activity level, and increase that activity while gaining more inner peace and enjoyment.

What is "Activity-Based Selling?"

The term "Activity-Based Selling" describes a specific type of sales where success is highly dependent on the number of prospects one contacts. In baseball, fielding statistics are computed based on the number of "chances" a player has to successfully field the ball. Success in Activity-Based Selling requires having a lot of chances. Examples of activity-based salespeople include: insurance agents, real estate agents, network marketers, and home-based business owners.

The opposite of Activity-Based Selling is "Strategy-Based Selling." In Strategy-Based Selling the sales representative sees only a few prospects in a given time period. It is the way he or she handles those few accounts that determines success. An IBM representative selling large computers to a major corporation is a strategy-based salesperson. He may work for a year on one sale, having multiple meetings, working with multiple decision makers, and guiding many small decisions that ultimately lead to a sale. He spends his time building relationships, trying to understand the client company's internal politics, and developing strategies to influence key decision makers. He has to be very careful because one false move can destroy many months or years of work.

By contrast, the successful activity-based salesperson sees a large number of prospects in a given time period. In this type of sale there is usually only one decision maker, the sales strategy is much simpler and is similar for each prospect. The activity-based salesperson's day is comprised of more traditional and repetitive sales activities including: prospecting, cold calls, and sales interviews. The higher the activity level in all these areas, the more successful an activity-based salesperson will be.

The Unique Challenge of Activity-Based Selling

Throughout my career as a salesperson I've been selling relatively small products to a large number of people. I'm an activity-based salesperson. And although I've always known activity level was a key to my success, I've sometimes struggled to maintain a consistently high level. There's nothing more frustrating than to know what you should do and then observe yourself not doing it. It seemed very hard to hold on to the consistent motivation I needed. In looking back I realized that many aspects of Activity-Based Selling are natural demotivators. Activity-Based Selling is uniquely challenging because, unlike other types of sales or other professions, the nature of the job can squash the very motivation that is critical to your success. Some of the more important demotivating factors include:

Independence

Unlike other jobs where a boss monitors your work, for the most part, activity-based salespeople are independent. Though many do have a manager, if they are compensated purely on commission, in essence they work for themselves. This independence requires that activity-based salespeople be continually *self*-motivated. I emphasize the word "self" because no one can force them to find prospects, make calls, and meet with clients. If they can't motivate themselves, no one else will.

Self-motivation may well be the most difficult challenge any human being will ever face. When I work with other people on a team, staying motivated to follow through on my commitments is relatively easy. But when I'm alone, when no one is depending on me but me, my motivation is significantly reduced. There is some kind of magic that occurs when two or more people work together on a project. They are accountable to each other and motivate each other. Self-motivation is difficult partly because this magic isn't present. Left alone, it is just too easy to stay where things are comfortable. Independence inhibits motivation because it is easy not to follow through on our commitments when we are only accountable to ourselves.

Insignificance of Tasks

Activity-based salespeople live in a world of tiny, little tasks that often seem insignificant: a phone call here, some paperwork there, a meeting there. By themselves, none of these tasks really matter that much. It's all these small tasks taken together over time that make a difference. Maintaining consistent motivation will be a real challenge if the tasks you are working on seem insignificant.

Rejection

Activity-based salespeople are constantly searching out and

contacting new prospects. And each contact carries with it a chance for rejection. As much as we've been taught that rejection doesn't matter, that it's not about us, and that we shouldn't take it personally, it still hurts. It's always more fun to interact with people who want to talk with you and who value what you have to offer. Even for the most seasoned sales veteran, rejection hurts. And because it hurts, it hinders motivation. Most of us don't want to do things that are painful, especially on a regular basis.

Low Yield

"Yield" refers to the percentage of prospects we contact who actually end up buying our product or service. "Low yield" means that in Activity-Based Selling, a significant percentage of prospects don't buy. In some businesses yield can be as low as 5-10%. Low yield causes frustration. It makes you feel like you are looking for a needle in a haystack. At the end of a long day it's easy to think, "Why bother? If so few people buy, why bother making a few extra phone calls, probably no one will buy anyway."

A continually high level of activity, which is the result of a continually high level of motivation, has to be present for an activity-based salesperson to succeed. Consistent motivation is hard for most people, but is uniquely challenging for activity-based salespeople because our jobs contain a number of factors that are natural inhibitors to motivation.

Rising to the Challenge

Based on what we've just covered, Activity-Based Selling looks like a pretty dismal profession. I've painted an unflattering, but I believe realistic, picture. However, don't let my woeful description of your avocation get you down. The value of making a realistic assessment of a situation is that it helps us know what to do about that situation. So what can we do about the abundant challenges of Activity-Based Selling? I believe there are several things.

First, realize that Activity-Based Selling is not hopeless. There are those who not only survive, but prosper in this challenging and uncertain profession. When you see them working, on the phone, mailing letters, and searching out prospects, they aren't hating every minute of it. They're loving it, they thrive on it. They aren't focused on what they will gain from their activity, they're having fun in the moment. There *are* ways to create activity that make it fun and free-flowing. We'll explore many of them in this book.

Second, we need to become curious observers of our own behavior, students of our activity. In the same way salespeople value product knowledge and persuasion skills as indispensable sales tools, we must learn to value *activity skills* as well. The skills needed to consistently "churn the numbers" are extremely valuable. Beliefs, work processes, and thought patterns are all aspects of the activity skills we will explore in this book.

Finally, we need to examine our own fears about activity. Imagine a large convention hall equally divided by a white line on the floor. On one side is the small group of salespeople who consistently make more calls, see more prospects, and submit more proposals than anyone else. On the other side is the huge crowd who struggle with producing the level of activity they know they need. Many people subconsciously fear that if they go over to the "other side" (the high activity side) they will never be able to come back, that their lives will become hectic and harried and completely devoid of fun. And it is this fear that keeps them with the crowd.

Our objective is not to create a life for you where you are always stressed, straining, and striving. If you're afraid of this, just keep in mind that you can always cross the line the other way if you choose. What we want is maximum productivity from the time you spend working. I want you to be able to work a *great* 40 hours, then leave it behind. Increased activity is actually going to increase your job satisfaction, reduce your stress, and most importantly increase your peace of mind.

A Word About "Motivation"

Since we will use the word "motivation" throughout this book, it is important that we clear up any confusion and ensure that we are using a common definition. Because of the great proliferation of motivational books, audio tapes, infommercials, and speakers, the word "motivation" is sometimes associated with hype or a momentary emotional high. A person who is experiencing this emotion is always smiling, talking a good game, expressing a "positive mental attitude," but not necessarily *doing* anything.

I want to make a clear distinction between the above definition and the one we will use. Throughout this book, the word "motivation" will be used in a very precise scientific context. Motivation is simply the force that causes you to act. With respect to self-motivation, we will use the following definition:

Self-Motivation: An inner force that compels behavior.[1]

The key word in this definition is *behavior*. Because we seek to manage behavior, we must understand and manage motivation. Motivation is an inner force (emotional, intellectual, spiritual, and/or physical) that sets an organism in motion. It is the precursor to all behavior. For the purpose of this book, we will consider motivation to be synonymous with behavior and having nothing to do with hype or some momentary emotional high.

About This Book

This book is constructed in three parts. Part I, *Understanding Activity*, defines the key benefit of increased activity, and describes the important beliefs and up-front planning necessary to maintain high activity. Part II, *Creating Activity*, is a collection of simple but powerful techniques that will help you get started on and follow

---

[1] Dennis Waitley, *The Psychology of Human Motivation*, (Chicago: Nightingale-Conant, 1992).

through with your important sales activities. And Part III, *Refining Activity*, analyzes the activity you've just created, looking for ways to streamline that activity and make it more effective.

Not So Sexy

There is a danger here that someone will think this book is about learning to work harder: making more calls, having more meetings, and mailing more letters. And let's face it, although you may need to do those things, it's not very appealing to learn to work harder. Who would want to invest time in that? I'd much rather learn to hone my persuasion skills or learn the latest negotiation techniques or learn to use my new contact management system. Those things seem a lot sexier than the blocking and tackling fundamentals required for creating more activity.

The truth is, this book would be very dry and boring it it were about working harder, *but it's not*. It's about working easier, having more fun, *and* generating more activity. There are those who regularly produce high levels of activity and don't think of it as work. If we can take on some of their work practices and thought processes, we too can be more relaxed, have more fun, *and* do more.

The strategies outlined in this book are things I've learned through both study and trial and error in my own career. Please keep in mind that what is contained in this book is only a beginning. This is not *the* answer. These are simply things my experience and research have shown to be very important in increasing and easing activity. I hope what we discuss in this book will cause you to think, ponder, and explore your own behavior and results. With respect to our careers, nothing will bring more satisfaction and contentment than continually increasing our competence and expertise. Ultimately, I hope you will develop your own theories and strategies for maximizing your comfort, activity, and peace of mind.

Part I:
Understanding Activity

Chapter 1
The Shortest (and Most Important) Chapter in This Book

"If we have not quiet in our minds, outward comfort will do no more for us than a golden slipper on a gouty foot."

-- John Bunyon

Compared to a car or a house or even a 747, the Hope diamond is very small ... but immensely valuable. Every woman who has ever received a diamond ring knows that sometimes valuable things come in small packages. Don't judge the value of this chapter by its size. In the next few pages I will address the infinitely important question of *why* you should even read this book. Don't miss this. And don't go forward until you understand it. The rest of this book is about how to increase your sales activity. This chapter is about *why* you should increase your sales activity. The greatest information in the world about how to do something isn't worth a darn if you don't have a clear *reason* to do it. With regard to developing your activity management skills, let me see if I can give you that reason.

There have been many days in my career as a salesperson where I could have done more than I was doing. Rest assured, my days were filled with activity. But in retrospect, it wasn't always *meaningful* activity. I may not have thought about it consciously, but at a subtle, subconscious level, I knew I could have done more than I was doing. This "subconscious knowledge" takes a tremendous psychological toll on a person. The greatest gift in life is to feel happy and contented from moment to moment. And this contentment can't exist with the knowledge that you have done less than you are capable of.

The obvious benefit from maintaining a consistently high activity level is that you will sell more. This is a worthwhile benefit, but I believe a secondary one. The primary benefit of increased activity is the feeling of pride and sense of peace you gain from knowing you have done all you can.

> *"You know what messes with the mind? Doing less than you can."*
>
> *-- Jim Rohn*

The real benefit of increased activity isn't what you gain from extending yourself, it's how you feel *because* you've extended yourself. Peace and contentment require that we use our skills fully in pursuit of some meaningful purpose. Psychologist Abraham Maslow called this "self-actualization," and said it was the highest need of all human beings. Meaningful activity that stretches our skills and talents is fundamental to inner peace.

Why do human beings need to maximize their talents? I don't know that I can explain it, but it seems logical. A racehorse yearns to run, a bloodhound longs to track, and a human being, whatever their talents, will feel unsettled unless they are using those talents fully. Unless we are *applying* ourselves, we feel like we are doing something wrong. And it's impossible to be happy with that feeling inside you.

We can define activity as "the daily work you do to generate sales" (making phone calls, writing letters, and seeing prospects). If you know you need to be doing these things and you're not doing them, or you're not doing them at the level you know you should be, you feel bad inside. Can you ever be truly happy with that feeling inside of you? Some people try to distract themselves so they don't have to face it, but this feeling, this subconscious knowledge, is always there, waiting to come out as soon as they try to have a quiet moment of peace. A large portion of our self-esteem is connected to how hard we are trying, to the effort we expend in pursuit of our goals.

If you are going to increase activity, you have to have a clear reason. I said I would give you one in this chapter. But first let me tell you what the reason is *not*.

Every sales manager, seminar leader, and motivational speaker will tell you you have to have *big* goals and dreams to motivate you. They tell you to put pictures on your bathroom mirror of the house or car or boat you want, and your desire to have these things will motivate you. I disagree. Dreams and goals *are* important, incredibly important, and you should definitely have them. But you've probably had a strong desire to have those things for many years. What makes you think that desire is going to motivate you now when it hasn't in the past? Do you want a reason that's going to drive you from minute to minute, hour to hour, and day to day for the next ten years as you stretch for those goals? Do you want a compelling "why?" Here it is.

If you do less than you are capable of, you are destroying your happiness, your contentment, and your peace of mind. You are dashing on the rocks any chance you have at life's most elusive, sought after, and precious gift: inner peace. And all the homes, cars, and boats in the world can't do a thing to replace that. Do what you know you must do because it's in you to do it. You are a human being, it's the way you were made, you have no choice. Learn to be the master of your activity not for the material possessions you will gain, but for sense of pride and inner peace that come with being the master of your own behavior.

The Need For Honesty

We all experience times when we aren't giving our best. During these times we often put up a front, sometimes without even thinking, to fool others into believing we're working harder than we really are. We talk about all the work we are doing: a meeting here, some paperwork there, the phone calls we have to make, and so on. But *you* know if you came in late, spent excessive time at the coffee pot chatting with your buddies, or squandered an inordinate amount of your selling time making personal phone calls. It may be okay to put up a front for others, but we have to be very careful that we don't fool ourselves. If we are ever going to learn to do more, we have to begin by honestly admitting that we could do more.

Reading this book will be a personal and confidential journey you and I take together. No one else has to know that you could be doing more than you currently are. But in the privacy of your mind, as you read this book, I will be asking you to be very clear with yourself about what you are currently doing and what you are capable of.

The people who will get the most from this book are those who are willing to admit they have observed themselves doing less than they know they are capable of doing; people who have observed this, yet have been unable to consistently get themselves up to their full potential. They know there is more inside, it just doesn't come to the surface as often as they would like.

A compelling why? A commanding reason for developing your activity management skills? It seems pretty simple. You have to look at yourself in the mirror every morning. Can you look deeply into those eyes and know that you have not done your best? Can you know that you have squandered opportunity, left money on the table, and literally let life slip through your fingers? Can you look at yourself daily, knowing all these things, and still be happy? You will have to answer that question for yourself, but I know I can't.

This book is about increasing your activity level, not so you will make more money, but so that you will be proud and feel good about the level of activity you generate every day. We spend a large portion of our lives involved in our jobs. It is essential to our overall happiness and sense of well-being that we feel good about the work we do. And the incredibly good news is, if you pursue excellence through activity for the purpose of gaining peace of mind, *fortune will come unsought.*

Chapter 2
It's Not All Discipline

*"My life seems like one long obstacle course,
with me as the chief obstacle"*

-- Jack Paar

In this chapter I want to convince you of one very important point, *getting yourself to produce consistently high levels of sales activity is not exclusively a matter of discipline.* Successful salespeople don't perform at high levels simply by forcing themselves to do things they dislike. The popular view is that those who make more calls, see more people, and do more paperwork than the rest of us do so because they are extremely disciplined. We tend to believe that these individuals experience the same lack of motivation as the rest of us, and through sheer willpower create high activity levels in spite of it. I want to offer an alternative view.

For the sake of this example, pretend you are a private in the Marine Corps and your drill sergeant has just ordered your company out on maneuvers. Your task is to travel from point A to point B in a thickly forested jungle. You are in competition with another company to see who can move through the jungle most quickly. Your company chooses one path, the other company chooses another. The path you have chosen leads in exactly the direction you want to go. It is easily traveled, but just as the end is in sight, you find a brick wall standing 15 feet high, for as far as the eye can see in either direction, right across the path.

Before you can decide what to do, your drill sergeant arrives, very angry, wanting to know what you're waiting on. You point to the brick wall. He says it's nothing. You're Marines, just break through it. He commands you to kick, hit, head butt, or do whatever it takes to break through the wall. Some of the members of your company reluctantly begin to follow his orders. They are kicking, pounding, and throwing themselves against the wall, all to no avail. They are falling down, bruised and bleeding, and the wall stands as strong as ever. How many times would you have to throw your body, bruised and bleeding, against this wall before you lost your enthusiasm for the exercise?

You hear a loud horn in the distance. The exercise is over. The other team has reached their destination because, unlike you, there was no brick wall in their path.

In this example, the brick wall is a metaphor for the mental obstacles that keep most of us from creating the level of activity we desire. The important distinction to be made here is this: the success of the high activity person is not exclusively due to their ability to break *through* brick walls. They have somehow gotten good at finding paths that don't have any, or as many, brick walls. It is not that they are better than the rest of us at overcoming task reluctance; because of the way they think, they don't experience *as much* task reluctance.

Our Thoughts Govern Our Activity

In every family there are a variety of personalities. We all have someone like Uncle Joe. Joe has been in sales for over 20 years, and during that time he has built his gift for gab. He is very comfortable striking up and carrying on a conversation with strangers. He is a good listener and has interesting stories to tell when it is his turn to talk. Every family also has someone like shy cousin Ben. He is easily embarrassed and finds it difficult to talk to relatives, much less strangers. Ben feels somewhat awkward about himself and has low self-confidence.

Imagine a new game show where participants are judged on their ability to meet and carry on a conversation with people they don't know. Contestants are placed in a large cocktail party with several hundred total strangers. They are monitored with video cameras and score points for the number of people they meet and with whom they strike up a conversation. If the two contestants competing against each other on this game show are Uncle Joe and cousin Ben, who would you put your money on?

Okay, so Joe is the obvious favorite, but let's think about this a little further. Would it be *impossible* for Ben to win? I submit that it would be *possible*, but extremely difficult. Trying to maintain a high level of meeting and talking with people would require much more effort and create a lot more stress for Ben than for Joe. But there are no *physical* limitations affecting these men's ability to meet and talk with people. Both have two legs, two arms, and a functioning set of vocal chords. If there are no physical limitations, then any limitations must be psychological. Right? The only difference *must* be the way these two men think about themselves and their situation.

Premise #1:

The way one thinks about himself and his situation determines the level of comfort he feels in that situation.

Ben's natural tendency in this scenario would probably be to stand in the corner and speak only when spoken to. If it were possible to help Ben think about meeting and talking with people differently, so that it was *more comfortable* for him, his ability to strike up a conversation would naturally increase. We will always produce more activity if it is comfortable rather than painful. This leads to our second premise:

Premise #2:

We do less of things that are uncomfortable for us.

Is it possible that generating consistently high levels of sales activity is more comfortable for some than for others? It seems that way. You probably know at least a few people who seem perpetually motivated, who stay passionate and excited about their work day-in and day-out, year after year. They are apparently immune to the internal struggles that plague most of us and destroy our motivation. Their motivation is not purely based on discipline. It comes from the fact that they are not facing as many mental obstacles as the rest of us.

We have just developed two key premises: our thoughts about a situation determine how comfortable we feel in that situation; and, our level of comfort governs our level of activity. From these two premises we can draw the following conclusion:

Conclusion:

Our thoughts govern our activity.

Getting Past the Walls

So it is our thoughts that either create or don't create the mental obstacles that block activity. And it is the existence of mental obstacles (not a lack of discipline) that keeps us from performing at high levels. If we use brick walls as our metaphor for mental obstacles, there seem to be three methods we can use to get past these walls.

Method #1: *Break Through the Walls*

Remember in our scenario that as soon as you hit the brick wall, your drill sergeant was there yelling at you to break through it, making you feel there was something wrong with you if you couldn't. Too often sales managers, sales trainers, and salespeople themselves play the role of drill sergeant. They say, "It takes discipline and hard work to be a productive salesperson. When it comes to making calls, you just have to sit down and *do it.*" They make you feel lazy or undisciplined if you don't. They are promoting what I call the Nike strategy for self-motivation, "Just do it!" What they are telling you is to act *in spite of* any fears or anxieties you might have about the task. This is the motivational strategy we will call "discipline, " acting in spite of fears and breaking *through* the mental obstacles that make a particular situation uncomfortable. While discipline would not be my choice for a *long term* self-motivation strategy, it does have its place. The ability to get yourself to do something even though you don't feel like doing it is part of being an adult. We all need some level of discipline, or else we would never do anything we didn't want to do. For this reason Part III of this book includes a chapter on understanding the nature of discipline and how to use it to our advantage.

Method #2: *Remove the Walls*

If you're standing by your desk, staring at the phone, and trying to get yourself to pick it up, you are facing a full blown case of task reluctance. In this case our drill sergeant coaches would say something like, "Hey, quit your belly aching, quit your complaining, and just sit your butt down and do your work." They never stop to consider that a better solution than throwing yourself against this brick wall might be to investigate what caused the wall and remove the cause, in essence making the wall vanish from your path. If you are having trouble picking up the phone, a good question to ask yourself is, "What's bothering me? What is it that is stopping me from doing what I know I need to do?" You might come to the conclusion that you are afraid of hearing the word "no," that hearing it would make you feel like a failure. In this case, a simple bit of logic may do the trick. Hearing a chorus of "no's" is much closer to success than never making any calls at all. Reminding yourself of this fact may be all the help you need to get yourself moving. It's much easier to get yourself into action by defining and dealing with obstacles than it is trying to act in spite of them. Throughout this book we will explore a number of methods for dealing with task reluctance after it appears. If applied, these techniques will remove much of the anxiety that makes a contemplated task uncomfortable. Successful salespeople perform at high levels in part because when they do face mental obstacles, they find ways around them rather than through them.

Method #3: *Prevent the Walls*

We've all heard the saying, "An ounce of prevention is worth a pound of cure." It is true that when obstacles exist it is better to remove them than it is to crash through them. But the best solution of all would be to prevent the walls from ever appearing. This is what truly high activity people do. They probably haven't thought of it consciously, but somewhere in their upbringing, they have taken on beliefs and habits that cause them not to experience the same task reluctance as the rest of us. And obviously, if you don't have as much fear or discomfort of a certain task, it's much easier to get yourself into action. In addition to learning about discipline and techniques for removing walls once they appear, in Part III we'll also explore a number of *preventative* techniques. In this case we'll be doing things to condition our mind and body so that when we arrive at a task we have significantly reduced task reluctance, and in some cases actually look forward to doing what was previously uncomfortable.

A Word of Warning

Throughout this chapter I've been emphasizing the point that activity is easier for some people. The thoughts that flow through the mind of the high activity person do not put up the same walls as the thoughts of the lower activity person. But in no way do I mean to indicate that we can abdicate responsibility for our actions, that we can say, "The reason he makes so many calls is because it is *easier* for him." Ultimately, we are all responsible for what we do. Some people have natural vocal talent. Singing is much easier for them than it is for the rest of us. But that doesn't give us the right to go to Carnegie Hall, stand on center stage and say, "Pardon me for singing out of time and off key. You see I wasn't born with natural singing talent. It's harder for me." If you weren't born with natural singing talent, and you want to sing at Carnegie hall, then you're going to have to work a little harder that those who were. We are all born with varying degrees of talent in different areas of our lives. If you have to work a little harder than someone else to develop your activity management skills, then you just have to work a little harder. No one is going to do it for you. The undeniable truth is, how much you do has *everything* to do with how much you sell. However you go about it, in the end we are all individually responsible for generating the level of sales activity we need to reach our goals. My purpose in writing this book is to show that discipline is not the only technique available for generating sales activity.

Why is Activity Easier for Some?

Why does high activity seem to be easier for some people than for others? Fundamentally it is because they think differently. *Our thoughts govern our activity.* High activity people have somehow developed thought processes that make high activity more comfortable for them than for most people. The successful don't just work harder (i.e. hit the brick wall harder), their thought processes make activity easier. Not easy, but easier. That's why meeting and talking to people is so much easier for Uncle Joe than it is for cousin Ben. If we are ever to reach our potential as activity-based salespeople, we must learn to manage thought in a way that frees up activity. That's precisely what the rest of this book is about.

If there is one thought I can leave you with from this chapter, it is this: *consistent motivation is not created by discipline alone.* Once and for all stop believing that the Uncle Joes in your office are tougher, meaner, or more disciplined than you; that they hate picking up the phone just as much as you, but through sheer willpower do it anyway. No one, I repeat NO ONE, stays continually motivated while throwing themselves against a brick wall. The greatest harm our drill sergeant coaches do to us is encourage us to believe all we need to do is work *harder* at self-motivation. I vehemently disagree. What we need to do is work somewhat harder and much *smarter.* If that sounds appealing, then keep turning the pages, you've got the right book in your hands.

Chapter 3
Enabling Beliefs

"For what a man would like to be true, that he must first believe."

-- Francis Bacon

It's very much in vogue today to make comparisons between our brains and computers. Computers make complex calculations, manage processes, and control machines with little or no human interaction. Through a process called "coding," programmers write the software computers use to control buildings, factories, and cities. "Beliefs" are the basic software around which our minds operate. Since the day you were born, your beliefs have been unknowingly coded by relatives, friends, and life experiences. Though you probably aren't aware of them, your beliefs have a profound impact on how you feel and behave every moment of every day. These beliefs operate at a subconscious level to mold and shape your thoughts, making high activity either more or less likely.

Because they operate at a subconscious level, most beliefs remain a mystery, even to the person who has them. The interesting thing about beliefs is that once they are established, rarely do we question their validity. Only when we experience a significant emotional event (loosing a job, getting a divorce, reaching a certain age) do we begin to question some of our core beliefs.

These subconscious beliefs are incredibly powerful because they control your behavior without your being aware of the source. Your reaction to an angry prospect, a lost sale, or a slow economy are all governed by beliefs. Because they control how you think and feel, beliefs have a huge impact on what you do.

A belief is a rule that determines how you interpret external events. I grew up in a fairly religious community in the South. Some of the members of our church had a belief that said, "Drinking is wrong." Whenever we would talk about someone drinking beer, or tasting wine, or anything having to do with alcohol, they would become very emotional and be visibly offended. Their belief controlled their feelings, and in a flash they were experiencing a full blown emotion without a second's conscious thought. Until they identified this belief and asked, "Do we really believe drinking is *wrong*?" it continued to have a major impact on their thoughts, feelings, and behavior. Beliefs, whether limiting or enabling, are powerful because they operate below the level of consciousness and at lightning speed. Examples of limiting beliefs many salespeople hold are: "I'm not good at asking for referrals," "I'm not very persuasive," or "It's tough to sell in a slow economy."

In this chapter I will present five beliefs critical to creating and maintaining high activity. If you disagree with any of the following belief statements, you're going to have a hard time. Even if you apply all the methods and techniques from the rest of this book, if you don't embrace these beliefs, you'll feel like something is holding you back. You may observe yourself behaving in a way you don't understand: coming in late, leaving early, or not making calls. The source of these behavioral problems will be hard to identify if your behavior is being controlled by beliefs operating below the level of consciousness. The first step to becoming a high activity salesperson is to integrate the following tenets into your own belief system. At the end of this chapter I'll give you some ideas about how to do that. For now, let's just look at what these enabling beliefs are. I call them "enabling" because they "make us able" to produce high activity. If you don't at some level embrace each of these beliefs, the chances of your being a highly active producer are ... well ... *highly* unlikely.

Enabling Belief #1

Activity level is a critical ingredient for sales success.

Seems pretty obvious, right? You have to believe activity is important before you'll be motivated to produce high activity. But who *wouldn't* believe that? You'd be surprised.

In interviews I've conducted with activity-based salespeople, some openly admit that they don't see activity as critically important. They think that persuasion skills, or product knowledge, or having the lowest price is what really matters. Activity level is not so important they say. Who knows, in certain circumstances they may even be right. I have to give them credit, at least they can state clearly what they believe. One thing we can be sure of is this: their lack of belief in the value of activity can only *hinder* them in producing high levels of sales activity.

Others openly state that activity *is* the key to success, but on the inside they question it. I've done this myself at times. Though I profess to be a staunch believer in the value of activity, sometimes, during a long dry period, I begin to feel like nothing I do matters, not increased activity, not increased effectiveness, nothing. The game of sales seems impossible to win. And as I allow this belief to creep into my mind, you can imagine what it does to my motivation.

To have any chance at becoming a highly active producer, you have to first believe in the value of activity. You have to believe, in your heart as well as in your mind, that if you see a large number of prospects, a certain percentage *will* buy.

Enabling Belief #2

Consistency makes activity easier and more effective.

This is an important belief if you are ever to make *consistent* activity part of your habit pattern. Activity is easier when spread evenly over a period of time. If your goal is to make 2600 calls a year, it is much easier to make 50 calls each week than to try and make 2600 in the last week of the year. Consistency is a great weapon in the pursuit of high activity. Playing catch-up is always harder.

Activity is also more *effective* when spread evenly over a period of time. Existing clients would probably rather hear from you once a quarter rather than four times in one week. Staying in touch consistently makes regular imprints in their minds. When they need your product or service again, or know of a friend who does, you will be the one on the tip of their tongue.

An additional benefit of contacting prospects regularly is that you keep your sales funnel continually filled, eliminating the huge ups and downs experienced by most salespeople. The more you believe in the value of consistency, the more likely you will be to produce the consistent activity needed to prosper in Activity-Based Selling.

Enabling Belief #3:

Success and failure occur in small steps over time.

Several years ago I conducted a seminar for gifted high school students. During the seminar we got into a lively discussion about what motivates people and what creates success in a person's life. At one point a student raised his hand and asked, "What is the formula for success?" I was surprised and impressed with the bluntness of his question. I responded by saying I could only share with him common attributes of high achievers. I would never be so arrogant as to say I had the "formula" for success. Later, while the class was busy doing an exercise, a shy girl pulled at my arm and said, "I know the formula for success." I smiled at her as she pointed down to her paper where she had written:

Success = Motivation x Time

She was saying that success, in whatever area we choose, comes from staying sufficiently motivated to take significant action over a long period of time. I had never seen it put quite that way before. And I had to agree with her that, as accurately as I had ever seen it, this was indeed the formula for success.

This formula is validated by anyone who has achieved greatness. Think of a modern sports hero like Michael Jordon. What do you think is responsible for his success? Clearly he was born with talent, but what *one event* made him great? In all those years of practice, was there one free throw, jump shot, or drive to the hoop that made him a superstar? OR, was it the *accumulated effect* of all those hours, days, and years of practice that over time turned a young boy with inborn talent into one of the preeminent sports celebrities of our time?

The ability to take advantage of the accumulated effect of small steps is available to us all. It is one of the hidden secrets to great success. Your motivation to take consistent action will be greatly enhanced if you believe that, in time, each small step layered one on top of the other *will* yield success.

Most people aren't motivated to take these small steps because they only want quick results. Unfortunately, in many cases because they aren't willing to take small steps, they end up not taking any at all.

"Nobody makes a greater mistake than he who does nothing because he could only do a little."

-- Edmund Burke

Enabling Belief #4

Work is good and a potential source of great pleasure.

I wish I always felt that way, but sometimes I feel like I shouldn't have to work so hard. I have friends with 9-to-5 jobs who seem to be doing very well. It's frustrating. Why should I have to work so hard when they don't?

There is a fundamental assumption underlying those feelings, the assumption is that "work" is something to be avoided. Surprisingly, when asked, few people describe great pleasure in their time away from work. Psychologist Victor Frankel used the term "Sunday Neurosis" to describe the lack of meaning his patients found in their days off. In his research on flow, author Mihaly Csikszehtmihalyi found that people had "optimal experiences" 54% of the time they were working, and only 18% of the time they spent in leisure activities. A team of Italian psychologists interviewed farmers living in mountain villages in Europe and reported that, "None of them drew a sharp distinction between work and free time. All mentioned work as the major source of optimal experience, [and] none would want to work less given the chance."[1] Most people in this country are preoccupied with leisure time. What a tragedy. It is this very preoccupation with leisure that robs us of much of the pleasure available through work.

The tasks that make up the day of an average salesperson (speaking to people on the phone, driving to and from appointments, and meeting new people) are things many people would *love* to have the opportunity to do. These tasks could even be thought of as fun. What a great thing to be in the middle of a sales interview, or making prospecting calls, and realize you were having *fun*. I've included a section in chapter 10 on how to make your time at the office more fun. For now, just begin to think about your work as a potential source of

---

[1] Mihaly Csikszentmihalyi, *Flow: The Psychology of Optimal Experience*, (New York: Harper & Row, 1990), page 158.

pleasure. If you believe work to be good and a potential source of pleasure, your chances of enjoying, and therefore prospering in, Activity-Based Selling will be greatly enhanced.

Enabling Belief #5

I can succeed and I will succeed.

This belief statement describes what is called a "high expected probability of success." Researcher John Atkinson believes that motivation is a combination of two factors: desire and expectancy.[2] In his writing, he defines *desire* as the degree to which we want some result, and *expectancy* as the degree to which we expect that our efforts will bring about that result. Most of us *expect* that we could get a job in a fast food restaurant, but aren't motivated to pursue it because we don't want a job in a fast food restaurant (i.e. our desire is very low). On the other hand, many people have a huge *desire* to have financial independence, but, because they don't expect that it's possible, rarely do they do anything about it. Motivation comes from having desire *and* an expectation that your efforts will lead you to the object of that desire. For most salespeople it is a lack of expectancy that is at the root of their problems with self-motivation.

If you don't have a high expectancy that you will succeed, then you are either uncertain of your success, or you out-and-out believe you will fail. Either of these thoughts will destroy your motivation. Why would you pour in the huge effort required for success if you are unsure that there will be any rewards? That wouldn't be rational. In order to stay motivated, you have to expect that you will succeed. Without this belief there is no reason for activity.

---

[2] Dennis Waitley, *The Psychology of Human Motivation*, (Chicago: Nightingale-Conant, 1992).

Of all the beliefs we've discussed, this is probably the most difficult one to fully embrace. It's easy to have doubts about your future success. The important message here is that the more you believe your efforts will lead to success, the more motivated you will be to produce those efforts. But how do you create this belief if you don't have it?

First, when you have an internal feeling of not wanting to do a specific task, realize that your lack of motivation may be because you are unsure that your efforts will pay off. When I am in this situation, I find it helpful to remind myself that uncertain success is better than certain failure. If I do nothing I am resigning myself to certain failure. If I try, if I take some action, at least I have a chance to succeed.

Ultimately, your belief in your ability to succeed will be based on your past successes. But this is a catch-22. It's like saying, "Which came first, the chicken or the egg?" If you haven't had success, you won't have the belief that will motivate you to take the action that will create success which will ultimately create the belief you needed in the first place.

So what's the answer? I'm sorry to say there is no easy answer. In the beginning you just have to move forward with faith that if you take proper action, it *will* yield good results. Try focusing on any small success you've had in your sales career or in any other area of your life. Let your motivation be ruled by your intellect rather than your emotions. Even if you're having a hard time believing in your heart, your intellect knows that if you do the right things, you *will* get results. And even your heart knows that if you do nothing, you won't get any results.

Identifying and Eliminating Limiting Beliefs

The first step in integrating these enabling beliefs into your belief system is to identify and challenge any limiting beliefs that contradict them. If you listen, you will hear belief statements surface in normal conversation. Individual beliefs are usually stated in a single sentence:

"I'm not good at asking for referrals."
"I could never make 100 calls a week."
"A slow economy has a negative impact on my sales."

If you want to identify someone's beliefs, when they make a statement ask yourself, "Is that a fact or a belief?" In almost all cases it will be a belief. People rarely speak in facts. Beliefs are generalizations, "I'm not good at asking for referrals." Facts are data specific, "The last three times I've asked for referrals I haven't gotten any." By listening for belief statements, you begin to develop a profile of the speaker's beliefs and therefore gain clues to their behavior. By developing a sensitivity to other's beliefs, you'll soon start to hear them in your own speech.

When you identify a negative belief, the best way to get rid of it is to immediately challenge it. When you hear yourself say or think, "I could never make 100 calls in a week," ask yourself if that's *really* true. Identify times in the past when you have done it or come close to doing it. Think about some of your colleagues who do it on a regular basis. If you can identify even one example that contradicts your negative belief, this will weaken it significantly. Challenge the belief every time you say or think it. Soon you'll begin to question whether the belief is valid. As you weaken your negative beliefs, you'll observe your behavior naturally conform to your new, more powerful belief system. Continue to monitor your thoughts and language and root out any negative or disempowering beliefs. Remember, *language indicates beliefs, beliefs determine behavior.*

Integrating Enabling Beliefs

If you don't hold at some level each of the enabling beliefs we've discussed, Activity-Based Selling is going to be an uphill battle. There are probably other important empowering beliefs, but I know these five to be critically important to creating and maintaining high activity. As long as you don't openly disagree with these beliefs, then just by seeing them stated explicitly, you have taken a significant step toward integrating them into your belief system. In order to further strengthen them, do the exercises that follow. Each of these exercises should take only a few minutes and is designed to integrate the beliefs into your day-to-day thought patterns. You should be able to do all of them over the next few days, but pick one and do it right now.

1. Write the five enabling belief statements on an index card. Review the card several times a day for the next three or four weeks. The act of repetition alone will begin to forge these beliefs into your subconscious.

2. Pick one of the beliefs and explain it to a friend. Do you understand it well enough to explain it clearly? Does your friend agree that it is an "enabling" belief? If he or she disagrees, can you convince him or her? The process of explaining and defending these beliefs will greatly enhance your commitment to them.

3. Listen for beliefs in one of the conversations you have today, preferably with a salesperson. For each belief you hear, ask yourself if it is an enabling or a limiting belief. How do you think it impacts this person's behavior? As you become attuned to listening for the beliefs of others, turn your attention to your own conversation. If you hear limiting beliefs, challenge them immediately using the technique from the previous section. Over time you should begin to hear fewer limiting and more enabling beliefs in your language.

Suggested Reading

Claude M. Bristol, *The Magic of Believing*, (New York: Pocket Books, 1948.)

Richard Gillett, *Change Your Mind, Change Your World*, (New York: Fireside Books, 1992).

Anthony Robbins, *Unlimited Power*, (New York: Fawcett Columbine, 1986), chapters 4 & 5.

Chapter 4
Defining Sales Activities and Target Levels

"The will to win is nothing without the will to prepare."

-- *John Wooden*

I know, I know, you're still waiting for me to get to the part where I tell you how to stay perpetually motivated, continually driven, and always active. You want to know how to create activity in a way that makes it easy and fun. But before we do that, we have to answer one final question: perpetually motivated to do *what*? Always active doing *what*? In this chapter we will answer the fundamental question facing all activity-based salespeople, "What must I do this day, this hour, and this minute so that when the end of the year arrives my goals will necessarily be realized?"

Every time I watch a sports event on t.v. and listen to an athlete analyze his or her performance, I am amazed at the level of detail to which they understand their sport. When I watch a sprinter run the 100 meters, to me it just looks like a person running very fast. To the runner however, the race is a series of discrete events: the placement of the feet in the starting blocks, the start, the lean of the body early in the race, the lean of the body later in the race, the cadence of the arms, the "kick" at the end, and the stretch for the tape at the finish line. All of these details are invisible to me, but for a professional athlete, understanding each of these things is critical to mastering their sport.

Why is it important for an athlete to have such a detailed understanding of their sport? Because in order to improve they must know where to focus; they must identify the areas that are holding them back and then work to improve those areas. It doesn't do any good for the track coach to say, "Run *harder*. Your problem is that you just aren't running *hard* enough." Only when the coach focuses on specifics can the runner make a meaningful correction, "Your run looks very good except the way you are positioning your feet in the blocks. Try placing your feet a little higher next time."

Anyone who wants to master their profession, whether they be a runner, a manager, an engineer, or a salesperson, can do so only by understanding and focusing on the components that make up that profession. If you want to become a master sales professional you must develop a detailed understanding of each of the components that make up your sales methodology. Only by mastering each of the steps can you hope to master the overall process.

Defining Your Sales Process

Just as a runner can define a series of steps he uses to run a race, a salesperson can define a *series of activities* he or she uses to generate sales. A typical sales process might look like this.

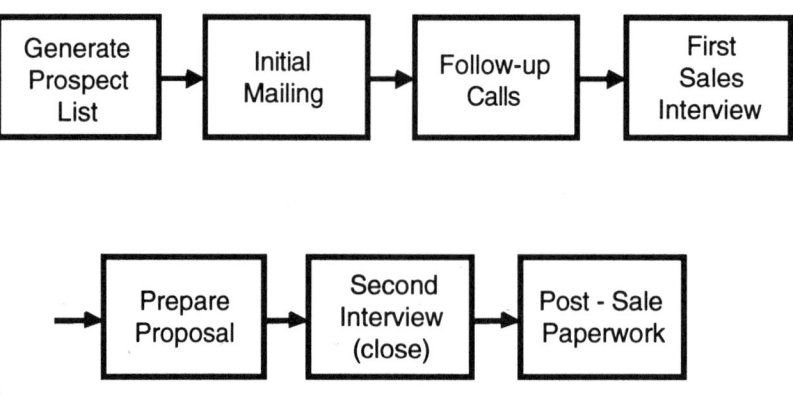

Figure 4.1: Typical Sales Process

The steps in your selling process will differ depending on your product, target market, and strategy. What's important is to have clarity about what those steps are. Note that the blocks in figure 4.1 describe generic, repetitive activities. Every step may not be used in every sale. Think of these as the activities you would engage in over the course of a year.

Developing a map of your selling process is a relatively simple task. Begin by thinking back over the past week and writing down everything you've done. What did you do Monday morning? Afternoon? Tuesday morning, etc.? When you've completed this list, group the things you've done into generic activities. Calling George to ask for referrals is part of "developing a prospect list." Submitting applications to underwriting is part of "post-sale paperwork," and so forth. Some of your activities will not be a direct part of the sales process. Weekly staff meetings or going to a sales seminar, though valuable, are not *directly* part of the activities that generate sales and therefore will not be included in the process map. One method for increasing your effectiveness may be reducing the number of activities you engage in which don't directly add to your bottom-line. Take a few minutes right now and sketch out your selling process.

Three Classes of Sales Activities

In preparing to manage sales activity, it's important to acknowledge that there are different types of sales activities. Looking at the sales process in figure 4.1, there seem to be at least three distinct types or "classes" of activities:

Class 1: *Discretionary (Pre-Interview) Activities*

The word "discretionary" means that you have a choice. With regard to sales activities, a discretionary activity is one you don't *have* to do. This may be a little unclear for some because I have labeled pre-interview activities (prospecting, phone calls, mailings) as discretionary. You could argue that these activities aren't discretionary at all because you have no choice, you *have* to do them. If you don't, you'll never sell anything. That's a good point. It is true that you have to do these things if you ever hope to sell anything. But the *level* at which you do them is completely your choice. There is no external pressure forcing you to work on your prospect list or pick up the phone. Any motivation to do these things must come from inside you. Because you aren't under the gun, your leverage, or desire to act, is often low for these activities. If you are the slightest bit uncomfortable with any of these activities, the tendency to procrastinate becomes extremely high.

Class 2: *Non-Discretionary Activities (Sales Interviews)*

The opposite of a discretionary item is a non-discretionary one. Sales interviews are non-discretionary because once they are scheduled you have no choice about if or when you do them. How many interviews have you missed because you just didn't feel like going at the time? When you are compelled by outside forces (i.e. someone is expecting you on a certain day at a certain time) your leverage, or desire to act, is very high. The tendency to procrastinate non-discretionary items is almost non-existent.

Class 3: *Semi-Discretionary (Post-Interview) Activities*

The third class of sales activity is what I call "semi-discretionary." These are items that have to be done, but you have some choice about *when* you do them. Semi-discretionary activities are usually those things that happen after a sales interview. Suppose you have your first meeting with a prospect on Tuesday. She is interested and requests a proposal, and you agree to a second meeting next Wednesday at which you will deliver the proposal. You have a fixed amount of time in which you can complete the proposal. It *must* be done by Wednesday, but because you have a choice about when you do it (i.e. any time before Wednesday), the tendency to procrastinate is high. However, because semi-discretionary items can't be put off indefinitely, we almost always find a way to get them done eventually.

Of the three classes of activities, discretionary activities are by far in greatest need of careful management. Non-discretionary and semi-discretionary tasks get done. Discretionary activities can be, and often are, put off indefinitely. Without careful tracking, it's easy to fool yourself into believing you're doing more than you really are. It's easy to get frustrated about why things aren't going well when the truth is you simply aren't keeping your pipeline full. It's vital that you manage discretionary tasks because they are the ones that get the ball rolling. Without them, nothing else matters.

Target Activity Levels: Process Goals vs. Results Goals

Results goals are very familiar to most salespeople. "I will list 3 new homes this month," "I will recruit 30 new people," "I will be the number one salesperson in the region," are all examples of results-oriented goals because they define the objective, or desired result, of your selling activities. They focus on the destination with no mention of the individual activities required to take you there.

Results goals are extremely important. Everyone should have them. We don't seek activity for activity's sake, but for the results it yields. You won't be able to create the high activity levels you want if you don't have a clear results-oriented *reason* for doing so.

The problem with having only results goals is that there are too many outside forces that can impact the result. A change in the economy, government regulations, company policies, or other factors beyond the control of the salesperson can have a tremendous impact (either positive or negative) on whether you reach your objectives. It's hard to stay consistently motivated when the rules of the game keep being changed by forces beyond your control.

Process goals focus on the one thing you have complete control over: your own behavior. As a real estate agent, it may not be within your control to sell exactly two new homes each month, but no one can stop you from identifying 20 new prospects, mailing 50 letters, and making 200 phone calls. These selling activities are all directly within your control. Process goals define the level of those activities that are the building blocks for your long term objectives.

"Sales Builders"

An Example of Process Goals in the Insurance Industry

Some insurance companies have monthly meetings for their producers called "sales-builders." The purpose of these meetings is to help agents build their client base. Approximately 8-10 agents voluntarily form a sales-builders group. The groups track the level of a standard set of process goals (finding prospects, making phone calls, closing sales, etc.), and each person reports on his or her activity and results each month. Group members hold each other accountable to continually perform at their target level for each activity. Though agents talk a lot about their effectiveness and how they are doing on their results goals, these meetings are essentially about holding people accountable to work the process. The underlying belief is: if you continue to find enough prospects and see enough people, eventually you will succeed.

In his book, *The Winner Within*, basketball coach Pat Riley relates a story of the 1986-87 season with the Lakers. They had lost the western conference finals the year before in a lackluster performance against the Houston Rockets. To kickoff the new season, the coaching staff initiated a new tracking system called CBE (Career Best Effort). CBE was an elaborate data analysis process which objectively compared a players performance with his best performance throughout his career. CBE didn't just measure results (points, rebounds, and assists), but effort (defense, shot contesting, shooting accuracy, etc.). As Riley said, he was trying to put a number on how hard his players were *trying*. Though some players fought this focus on the details, over time they came around. By forcing the team to focus on the building blocks for success, CBE helped the Lakers rebound from their defeat the previous year and win the NBA Championship over the Boston Celtics.

The Lakers Career Best Effort system is really a method of creating and tracking *process goals.* A process goal is a target for the interim steps in a process rather than the end result of the process. The idea is that if you do all the steps right, the results will take care of themselves. In talking about CBE Riley said, "We didn't know if we could win, but we knew we could develop *winning habits."* Whether external events are helping or hindering your progress toward your desired result, a focus on process goals will ensure that you are doing everything within your power to create the result you are after. Setting and reaching process goals is a "winning habit" we can all benefit from.

> *"Excellence is the gradual result of always striving to do better."*
>
> -- Pat Riley

When defining target activity levels, there are three types of process goals you may want to use:

Type 1: *Amount*

The first type of process goal is called "amount." This is when you set a goal for a certain amount of something: phone calls, letters, number of new prospects, etc.

Examples: "I will make 50 phone calls each week."
"I will find 20 new prospects each week."

Note that the examples above are something over which you have absolute and total control. No one can stop you from going out and finding twenty new names. No one can stop you from picking up the phone fifty times. Moving slightly toward a results-oriented goal, you could choose to set a goal for the number of decision makers you talk with each week, or the number of meetings you schedule. Though it may be appropriate to choose these as your process goals, be aware that you are moving away from what you can absolutely control. If decision makers are not in their office when you call, you can't talk to them. Your ability to schedule a meeting will depend on their schedule as much as on your effort or your sales ability.

Type 2: *Length of Time*

The second type of process goals is what's called a "length of time" goal. Instead of choosing a fixed number of something, we define a fixed amount of time we will spend doing it. Length of time goals work well for activities where there can be a great variation in the number of hours required to accomplish a fixed amount. Sometimes finding 20 new prospects may be relatively easy, other weeks it may take 40 hours. Instead of finding 20 new prospects each week, it may be more reasonable to set a length of time goal.

> *Example:* "I will invest two hours each week in developing my prospect list."

Type 3: *Time Limit*

The third type of process goal is called a "time limit" goal. Time limit goals limit the amount of time you can delay doing a task after the need to do that task arises.

> *Example:* "I will have all applications completed and to underwriting within two days of closing the prospect."

Some steps in the sales process don't lend themselves to amount or length of time goals. To say, "I will complete three proposals per week" is of little value if you don't have three prospects who request proposals. Another week you may have eight proposals due. In this case saying, "I will work two hours per week on proposals," isn't appropriate either. This is where a time limit goal works well. Using a time limit goal you would say, "I will complete each proposal within two days of the request." This type of goal is very useful because it allows your work volume to fluctuate as needed. Time limit goals work well for post-interview activities where the needed volume of the activity varies from one week to the next.

What is the Appropriate Level for Key Sales Activities?

A question that often arises at this point is, "How do I know the appropriate level for my key sales activities?" The answer is simple, whatever level is required to meet your sales objectives. Target activity levels are something you experiment with and adjust based on experience. If your objective is to make two sales per week and 20 calls per week only generate one sale, increasing your calls to 40 per week should result in two sales.

Most adults know how to read a road map. Even though they may take a wrong turn here or there, given enough time, they always find their destination. In sales, your objectives are your destination. Target activity levels are the road map that take you there. By clearly identifying and monitoring sales activities, you can adjust the level of those activities until you hit your target.

Time Frame: When to Reset the Score on Process Goals

An important point to consider here is the appropriate time frame for a process goal. Should the goal be to make 5,000 phone calls per year, 400 per month, 100 per week, or 20 per day? The time frame for process goals defines when you "reset the score" or when you wipe the slate clean and start over.

Suppose I choose a weekly time frame for my process goals. If my goal is to make 50 calls per week and in this particular week I only make 25, my goal for next week is *not* 75, it's still 50. If I make 75 calls instead of 50, my goal for the next week is *not* 25, it's still 50. At the end of the week I wipe the slate clean. By definition, the count for a *weekly* process goal starts over again each week.

I have a strong preference for setting process goals weekly. Monthly goals work for some people. Daily goals work for others. I have found that weekly process goals work *much* better for me. For me, a monthly goal doesn't put enough pressure on during the first few weeks of the month, and daily goals can sometimes be missed because of unexpected occurrences. I do have daily targets, they just aren't set in stone. If my goal is to make 50 calls a week, then obviously I need to average 10 calls a day. But "ten calls per day" is *not* the goal. If I have sales interviews that keep me out of the office most of the day Monday, I don't feel bad if I don't make any calls. I just know I need to make a few more each day to catch up. Having weekly goals makes me feel more like I am playing a game I can win. It feels like a football game that has five quarters. (I know, there can really only be four *quarters*. But give me some room, I'm exercising my poetic license here.) It's like I'm playing the Pittsburgh Steelers and I'm a few points behind at the end of the first quarter. It actually feels like a game, and the challenge to come from behind makes it exciting. On the other hand, if I know I will be out of the office Thursday and Friday, then I know I have to work hard Monday thru Wednesday. In this case there is an element of planning and strategy to achieving weekly goals that makes it fun for me. I like weekly goals because they exert enough pressure to keep me motivated, but when something unforeseen does come up, I still have time to recover. If I only had specific daily goals, I would just miss them and feel bad about it. It's harder to control the events of a day than a week.

Some people would not support my philosophy of resetting the score. They would say that if you miss your goal by 25 calls, the goal for the next week *should* be 75. I disagree. The concept of time frame is extremely important because if you're going to maintain motivation, you must set the game up so you can win. You want to be adequately challenged but not overwhelmed. If your goal is to make 50 calls per week and you miss that goal by 25 calls for six weeks, without resetting the score, your goal would become 200 calls in the current week. With this philosophy your goals can pile up until there is no possibility for success. And when there is no possibility of success, there is no motivation. In the NFL they don't carry over the score from one game to the next. In my opinion, neither should we.

CONGRATULATIONS!!!

Just by reading this far into this book you've already accomplished more than 95% of the people who buy self-improvement and business books. In this chapter you've at least read through, and hopefully worked through, some extremely important concepts on defining what you want to accomplish and how you plan to do it. This type of detailed planning is not something most salespeople enjoy, but you've done it and I compliment you for that. You have laid the groundwork for becoming a master of your own activity. But if you view the planning process as difficult I've got some bad news: making a detailed plan for your activity is the easy part. Now comes the hard part, executing your plan. In Part II, we'll explore a number of specific methods and techniques for managing your motivation so that executing the activities you have defined, and therefore reaching your long term goals, will move from the realm of hope and chance to the realm of certainty.

Application Exercises:

If you haven't done these exercises as you were reading the chapter, stop and do them now before you go on to Part II.

1. Define your sales process. Sketch out a process map with the typical activities you would engage in over the course of a year. Only include activities that are directly related to making sales.

2. Identify your "key" sales activities. In looking at your sales process, identify as key activities those which are critically

important and/or where you sometimes lack needed motivation. Concentrate on pre-interview activities.

3. Set process goals, either amount, length of time, or time limit, for each of your key sales activities.

Part II:
Creating Activity

Introduction to Part II
Creating Activity

In chapter 4 you defined your sales process and target levels for each of your key sales activities. The key question now (and the real focus of this book) is how to consistently hit the targets you've set. In chapter 1 I told you one of the fundamental questions of my life is, "How do I get myself to do what I know I should do?" The techniques in this part of the book are my attempt to answer that all important question.

Some of the ideas presented in Part II are specific techniques, others are shifts of attitude or philosophy that tend to ease activity. These techniques are not meant to be used all at once. You should choose two or three that appeal to you and experiment with them. If they work, keep them. If not, try some others. You may find as you read these ideas that they trigger some of your own. Feel free to borrow, adjust, and refine these techniques to create new ones that work for you.

Our ultimate destiny in life will be determined by how we stack our days one on top of the other. We want to get from each day the very most it has to offer. The techniques in Part II are designed to help you do just that.

Chapter 5
Health and Vitality

"Fatigue makes cowards of us all."
-- Vince Lombardi

When was the last time you woke up feeling great? A day where you woke up with lots of energy and felt like you had the world by the tail? On those days the air smells a little sweeter, the world looks a little brighter, and there is a little more bounce in your step. We've all had at least a few of these days and we'd all like to have more of them. What impact do you think feeling that way has on your ability to create effective sales activity? Isn't it easier to make phone calls, do paperwork, and handle rejection when you are feeling energized than when you're feeling lethargic?

Think back to a day where you didn't feel so great. A day where you woke up with very little energy, a day where you felt like the world had you by the tail. The air didn't smell as sweet, the world didn't look as bright, and the bounce was gone from your step. We've all had plenty of days like this and we'd all like to have fewer of them. What impact does feeling that way have on your day at the

---

Special Note: Although the author and publisher have exhaustively researched the information contained in this chapter, we assume no responsibility for errors, inaccuracies, omissions or any inconsistency herein. Readers should use their own judgment or consult a medical expert or their personal physician for specific applications to their individual problems.

office? Isn't it more difficult to make phone calls, do paperwork, and deal with tough prospects when you are feeling tired and sluggish than when you're energized? Trying to be productive on days like this can feel like trying to dribble an under-inflated basketball.

A person's physical energy has a colossal impact on their productivity. This is doubly true for independent salespeople who have to maintain continual *self*-motivation to succeed at their jobs. Physical vitality is a pivotal element in maintaining self-motivation. Feeling energetic may not solve all your problems, but without physical energy there is little hope that you will be highly productive. If you had the greatest strategy in the world, but no physical vitality, your plans wouldn't take you very far. To think that you could do tremendously well in sales without high energy is simply not logical.

The dictionary defines vitality as: "physical or mental vigor; power of enduring; lively and animated character." For our purposes we will define vitality more simply as, "the internal feeling that helps you think, react, and perform." The concepts and principles contained in this chapter have one purpose, increasing that internal feeling. It happens to be a bonus that doing things that increase your vitality, in almost all cases, also improve your general health. You can be confident that when you change your diet, exercise habits, or sleep habits, for the purpose of increasing your vitality, you will also be improving your overall health (i.e. stamina, emotional outlook, longevity, and resistance to disease).

The reason increasing vitality also improves health is that vitality is the natural state for the human body. When you are feeling less than energetic it is likely that you are mentally or physically doing something to block your natural state of vitality. Most of the techniques in this chapter are meant to remove the self-inflicted barriers to your natural energy state. By returning to a more natural state (removing stress, removing toxins in your environment, getting enough sleep) it follows that you will also be improving overall health.

One of the most important aspects of energy management is to have realistic expectations. Before we begin talking about energy management techniques, we should acknowledge the fact that different people have different levels of natural energy. While it is not natural for anyone to feel fatigued and drained all the time, it is reasonable to expect that some people will have higher energy levels than others. Human beings come in all shapes and sizes: short, tall, fat, skinny, blonde, brunet. Since we all have varying external characteristics, it is logical to assume we have varying internal characteristics: metabolism, insulin levels, hormone production, and so forth. We all know people who live on the lower end of the energy continuum. They move more slowly, talk more slowly, and get less excited than others. It would be hard to imagine one of these people changing dramatically into a super-high energy person. They just aren't built that way. Begin your energy management program with realistic expectations. Expect to maximize your energy level within your natural range, not to move from one energy range to a dramatically different one.

The ideas presented in this chapter are not a prescription. I will not lay out the perfect diet or exercise program and admonish you to follow it. I will simply present ideas for you to consider that are important for maximizing your energy. This chapter will give you the information you need to develop your own high energy program. I want you to understand these methods and techniques, apply them, and observe the results. When you get favorable results, keep that element as part of your overall energy management program. If a particular technique doesn't help you much, move on to something else.

However you go about it, we all need to maximize our own natural energy state. One thing we can say with absolute certainty is that we function better when we have physical vitality than when we don't. The key question is how to get more of it. This chapter attempts to answer that all important question.

Energy Drains

We will now take a look at some things that may be blocking your natural state of energy and vitality. By removing some of these barriers you can begin to enjoy the intoxicating feeling of healthy, vibrant energy.

Sleep Deprivation

> *"Thirty-eight million Americans (17% of the population) report that they have trouble falling asleep at night, and seven percent of us actually rely on medication to fall asleep."*[1]

I have to admit that when I began doing research on the causes of fatigue I was surprised to find in almost every reference a chapter on sleep disorders. I was surprised because I thought as a cause of fatigue, not getting enough sleep would be blindingly obvious. If you stay up till 3:00am, or can't sleep all night because the neighbor's dog is barking, of course you'll feel tired the next day. You don't need a Ph.D. to figure that one out. But it turns out not to be so obvious. Sometimes people who are fatigued during the day due to sleep disorders don't realize they are experiencing a sleep related problem.

> *"Patients who are suffering from sleep disorders often believe they are sleeping enough and sleeping well."*
> -- *Dr. Ronald Hoffman*

There seem to be two primary areas of sleep problems: not getting enough sleep, and not getting restful sleep.

On the subject of not sleeping enough, the first question that comes to mind is, "What is enough?" That's a tough question to answer because it can vary radically from one person to the next. One author

---

[1] Ronald L. Hoffman, *Tired All The Time: How to Regain Your Lost Energy*, (New York: Poseidon Press, 1993), pg 157.

reports that the range of needed sleep is from 4-10 hours. No one knows why, but some individuals seem to function very well, *on an ongoing basis*, on as little as four hours sleep. Others need as much as ten. The average person needs somewhere between 7-8. Note that I said functions very well on *an ongoing basis*. Anyone can function on four hours of sleep for a day or two or even three, but then we collapse, fall apart, and need to sleep late in order to catch up. The key question is what is the *steady state* amount of sleep you need so you don't fall apart and have to catch up.

One clue to whether you are getting enough sleep is how much you sleep on the weekend. If you sleep much later on Saturday and Sunday than you do during the week, chances are that you are not sleeping enough Monday through Friday. Another way to find out how much sleep you need is to observe how many hours you sleep when you are 4-5 days into a vacation. By that time you should be caught up on any sleep deprivation and, assuming a relatively stress free vacation, you should be sleeping according to your physical needs. The real, ultimate test of whether you are getting enough sleep is whether you wake feeling refreshed. If you wake feeling tired or lethargic, assuming that you have slept soundly, you probably haven't slept enough. If you feel you aren't getting enough sleep, try going to bed an hour earlier and see if you feel better in the morning. Experts report that for improving vitality, getting to bed earlier is more effective than sleeping later.

The second sleep related problem is restless sleep. We may spend plenty of hours in bed, but not be sleeping restfully. Each of us goes through a sleep cycle lasting approximately one and a half hours. During that time we move from light levels of sleep to progressively deeper levels. Getting to the deep levels is important, and waking during the night interrupts this process. Most people wake 2-3 times a night but fall back asleep so quickly that they don't remember it. One patient who suffered from chronic fatigue felt she was sleeping well, but was sent by her doctor to a sleep disorder clinic. There she was monitored as she slept and found that she suffered from sleep "apnea," or interrupted sleep. Researchers noted that she woke over 200 times in a night. The amazing thing is that she fell back asleep so quickly that she never remembered waking, and therefore had no idea her fatigue was related to a sleep disorder. It turned out she was a great snorer, and it was her snoring that kept waking her up. She was fitted with a snore guard and her problem was solved.

If you suspect restless sleep as a cause of fatigue, try the following:

Make sure your bedroom is completely dark. Release of the neurotransmitter melatonin (which causes drowsiness) is triggered by darkness. Use eye covers if necessary.

Make sure your sleep environment is as quiet as possible. If necessary use earplugs.

Try sleeping on your side if you suspect that your sleep is interrupted by snoring. If the problem persists, investigate an antisnore device called a "snore-guard" (for more information contact Dr. Donald Rosebloom (201) 845-8411).

See a sleep specialist. If you think you have further problems regarding restless sleep, ask your doctor to recommend a sleep disorder clinic.

Depression

Depression has been called the common cold of mental health. It is estimated that at any point in time thirteen million people suffer from some form of depression in the United States. Experts predict that one in five Americans will suffer a major bout of depression in their lifetime. As common as it is, depression is still one of the most misunderstood mental conditions we experience.

For me the word *depression* used to conjure up an image of a middle aged, out of shape, apathetic man sitting in a darkened room in the middle of the afternoon with a drink in one hand, a t.v. remote in the other, hoping very much that tomorrow never comes. I thought that people who let themselves get to that level of depression were "weak minded." Because of this distorted concept of what it meant to be depressed, it was a word I refused to apply to myself, even though at times it would have been very helpful to admit what I was feeling.

While the image described above may be an accurate depiction of severe depression, it is far from an accurate image of the kind of depression most of us face. For the sake of our discussion, we will define depression as follows:

Depression: *a feeling of apathy, a loss of interest or pleasure in usual activities, a lack of ability to think clearly and concentrate.*

The mild case of depression that you and I typically experience is not something that requires antidepressant drugs or time on a psychiatrist's couch to overcome. For most of us, our mild form of depression lasts at most 2-3 days and then we come out of it on our own. It is part of the natural cycle of moods all human beings experience.

Whole books have been written about depression and its various causes. I'm not going to try to answer in a few paragraphs questions experts struggle to answer in an entire book. My only purpose for discussing depression here is to identify it as a significant energy drain. One symptom that invariably accompanies depression is fatigue. And fatigue is the antitheses of the high physical energy that is critical to being a good salesperson.

So, what can you do? How do you fight depression and the fatigue that accompanies it? The first thing is to recognize when you are feeling depressed. As with any problem, awareness is the first step to a cure. That's why it was so harmful for me to refuse to admit I was depressed. If I wouldn't admit it, there was no chance I was going to take steps to correct it. Keep an eye out for the telltale symptoms: apathy, a lack of energy, sleepiness and fogginess, and difficulty in concentrating. Though these symptoms may be caused by something else, depression is a likely cause for otherwise healthy people.

When you recognize yourself in a mildly depressed state, try the following:

Exercise. If you don't currently have a regular exercise program, now might be a good time to start. If you do exercise regularly, don't let depression throw you off your routine.

Avoid ruminating over the problem that triggered your depression. Try not to keep thinking about the rude prospect who just abused you on the phone. Try to get some perspective by talking to someone else about what's bothering you.

Attack the problem. Rather than hiding from it, go do something that will solve the problem that triggered this bout of depression. Get lost in "doing" and you'll soon feel much better.

Give yourself a mini-vacation. Maybe what you need is a break. Take a half day off and do something you wouldn't normally do. Go to the zoo, call an old friend, take your spouse out to a movie.

Look for humor in the situation. Humor is always a universal antidote for melancholy feelings. Try to find something funny about the situation. Talk to a friend who makes you laugh.

It's important to note that we are not talking about severe depression. If you suspect that you are suffering from severe depression, see your doctor. What we've been talking about are the mild cases of depression we all face from time to time and how you can minimize their impact.

Energy Draining Dietary Habits

In a society that celebrates thinness, we usually think of dietary control as a means to weight loss. *Stop thinking that way.* At least for the next few minutes. In this section I want to encourage you to carefully choose what you put in your mouth, *not* to reduce your waistline, but to increase you vitality (which ultimately will increase your *bottom*-line).

The dietary choices you are making may unknowingly be robbing you of precious energy. The human body is designed to be healthy and energetic in its natural state. The dietary choices I will be asking you to consider will increase your energy by returning your body to a more natural state. The good new is, if you return to a more natural state, you can be confident that you will also reduce your waistline.

Making dietary changes can be very rewarding as a method of energy management because significant gains in energy can be made relatively quickly. By altering your diet slightly you can feel significantly better in as little as 24 hours. But controlling your diet can also be a formidable task. Most of us use food for relaxation and entertainment as much as a source of nutrition. And because we use food for relaxation and entertainment, modifying your diet can feel like a major lifestyle change ... one many people are unwilling to make, even for the promise of greater energy.

Because adopting totally new dietary habits can be an ominous task, I'm not going to prescribe an ideal diet and then implore you to follow it. I'm simply going to ask you to conduct an experiment. Over the next few weeks I'd like you to make some minor changes in your dietary habits and then monitor your energy level. If a particular dietary change increases your energy, then consider adopting it as part of your overall energy management program. If one of these suggestions doesn't work for you, then set it aside. And don't feel you have to religiously adhere to something just because it works. Even though reducing the amount of sugar in your diet may increase your energy, you may decide that this is a sacrifice you are unwilling to make. That's okay. My purpose here is not to make you feel guilty for what you eat. I just want to raise your awareness so you can make better choices.

Nutritional literature is fraught with inconsistencies. One reference says "eat this and don't eat that," another says "eat that and don't eat this." What is a person to do? I am convinced the only way we can make any sense of it all is to experiment for ourselves. The following are some of the common principles and leading theories from nutritional literature. I would like you to experiment with some of these over the next few weeks:

Eat less fat. The average American gets 40% of the calories in their diet from fat. The USDA recommends that no more than 30% of our daily calories come from fat, and most experts say we should shoot for 20%. Fat saps energy by reducing the ability of red blood cells to carry oxygen (a basic building block for energy) to the rest of the body. By reducing the fat in your diet, you increase oxygen and therefore energy.

A gram of fat contains approximately 9 calories. You can monitor your fat intake by reading nutritional labels and calculating the percentage of calories that come from fat. For example:

NUTRITION INFORMATION
SERVING SIZE . . . . 6 oz SERVINGS PER CONTAINER 4
Amount per serving CALORIES . . . . 100 PROTEIN (grams) . . . . 2 CARBOHYDRATE (grams) . . . . . . 14 FAT (grams) 6

$$\% \text{ Fat} = \frac{6 \text{ grams} \times 9 \text{ calories per gram}}{100 \text{ total calories}} = 54\%$$

The percentage of fat in this food is 54%. This is not necessarily a problem as long as your *overall* fat intake for the day is in the 20-25% range. If you reduce the amount of fat in your diet, over time you'll experience an increase in energy and a noticeable reduction in your waistline. Keep in mind, foods highest in fat include: red meat, butter, oils, cheese, and nuts. Foods lowest in fat include: fruits, vegetables, and grains. Also, experiment with some of the new low-fat or fat-free foods available in your supermarket.

Eat Less. Not only do Americans eat too much of the wrong things, they also eat too much. Since a huge percentage of your energy (up to 50%) is consumed in the process of digestion, the more food you have to digest, the less energy you will have for other things. An average man weighing 150 pounds needs approximately 2,200 calories to maintain his weight. A woman weighing 125 pounds needs approximately 1,800 calories. Of course calorie requirements vary according to body weight, metabolism, exercise habits, and other factors. If you are consuming more calories than you need, not only are you adding to your waistline, you are reducing the energy you have available for work.

Eat more fruits and vegetables. Aside from being low in fat, fruits and vegetables provide almost perfect nutrition for the human body.

> *"All the nutritional requirements that the human body has - all the vitamins, minerals, proteins, amino acids, enzymes, carbohydrates, and fatty acids that exist, that the human body needs to survive - are to be found in fruits and vegetables."*[2]

Fruit requires the least digestive energy of any food you can eat. While it can take up to eight hours for an average meal to leave your stomach, fruit passes through in 20-30 minutes. Any energy that is not used in digestion is freed up for work or play. A diet that requires less energy for digestion is a high energy diet.

Because you want fruit to pass through your stomach quickly, you should always eat it on an empty stomach. One way to ensure this is to follow the "fruit-till-noon" principle described by Harvey and Marilyn Diamond in their book, *Fit for Life*. The fruit-till-noon principle simply says you should eat nothing other than fruit from the time you wake until your noon-time meal. This is because from the hours of 4am-12noon your body is going through its elimination cycle, eliminating food that was eaten the day before. Eating concentrated, hard to digest foods during this time will disturb the body's natural process of elimination

---

[2] Harvey and Marilyn Diamond, Fit For Life, (New York: Warner Books, 1985), page 36.

and require more energy.

I've tried the fruit-till-noon principle myself and experienced great gains in energy. If you crave carbohydrates as I sometimes do, try supplementing the fruit with a small muffin or some toast. If you're not willing make such a dramatic change to your morning routine, try eating one piece of fruit (apple, orange, banana, etc.) as your first food of the day and then wait 20-30 minutes before eating anything else. You'll see some benefits even with this lesser approach.

Vegetables are a natural source of vitamins and minerals and are naturally low in calories and fat. Among their other benefits, vegetables provide an abundant amount of fiber. The benefits of fiber are many, from increased regularity to reduced risk of some types of cancer.

The less you cook your vegetables the better. Fresh vegetables are better than frozen, frozen better than canned. Eat them raw whenever possible, and when you do cook them, lightly steam them as opposed to boiling. One easy way to increase the amount of vegetables you eat is to have a salad with almost every meal.

Explore the art of juicing. In the hectic pace of our lives today, sometimes it's hard to find time to eat the recommended 4-5 helpings of fruits and vegetables. An easy and enjoyable way to get the benefits of eating fruits and vegetables is juicing. Drinking freshly squeezed juices is not a substitute for eating fruits and vegetables, but it is a good supplement. There are two types of juicers available, citrus juicers and vegetable juicers. Citrus juicers have a cone that turns and allows you to get juice from citrus fruits like oranges, grapefruits, and lemons. A vegetable juicer allows you to extract a surprising amount of juice from carrots, celery, apples, broccoli, and other vegetables you would have never thought of as "juicy." The good news is, today you can experiment relatively cheaply. With the recent wave of juicing, you can now find small vegetable juicers in most department stores for as little as $30.

Eat protein for alertness, carbohydrates to relax. In her book, *Managing Your Mind and Mood Through Food,* Judith Wurtman discusses the connection between food and the production of brain chemicals called neurotransmitters. These chemicals effect how brain cells, called neurons, communicate with each other and therefore how alert or non-alert we feel. Wurtman explains that eating protein produces the neurotransmitters dopamine and norepinephrine, responsible for alertness. Carbohydrates (sugar, bread, pasta) produce seritonin, creating a calming effect. A good idea is to emphasize proteins at lunch to enhance your alertness in the afternoon, and carbohydrates at dinner to help you relax as bedtime approaches.

These are just a sampling of the ideas and techniques you'll find in the literature on nutrition. Even though you'll be frustrated by the inconsistencies and contradictions, I recommend that you read more about diet and nutrition on your own (see the references list at the end of this chapter).

Circadian Rhythms

Certain physiological aspects of the body have regular patterns of variation throughout the day. Heart rate, blood pressure, and temperature are lowest in the morning and then rise and fall slightly at different points during the day. This pattern of variation is very similar from one 24 hour period to the next and is known as *circadian*, or daily, rhythms.

We don't just have circadian rhythms for physical measures like heart rate and blood pressure, we also have regular patterns of waking, eating, sleeping, *and* physical energy. Our alertness, or feeling of vitality *naturally* waxes and wanes throughout the day. This waxing and waning of alertness is such a common phenomenon that the music company Muzak, which provides background music for offices across the country, plays more upbeat music between the hours of 10:00am and 3:00pm, the times when most people feel lethargic and drowsy.

You might ask, "Is there anything I can do about these fluctuations?" The short answer is "No." Your energy will always be cyclical. Although you can take measures to raise your overall energy level (that's what this chapter is about), you will never completely eliminate energy fluctuations. What you *can* do is structure your work to make the most of your peak energy times. My most alert time of the day is from 5:30am to about 10:30am. That's when I do my best writing, thinking, and organizing. I have the least energy in the afternoon between the hours of 3:00pm and 5:00pm. Because I'm aware of my circadian rhythms, when I have a choice, I keep my mornings clear for working in my office and schedule sales calls and client meetings in the afternoon. Not only does the stimulation of interacting with other people during the afternoon perk me up, but scheduling meetings in the afternoon is also helpful because they are a "non-discretionary" activity. Once I've scheduled them, I have no choice, I *have* to show up. If I schedule discretionary tasks (paperwork, making cold calls, etc.) during the afternoon, my tendency to procrastinate is much greater. My most productive days are those where I work in my office in the morning and have meetings in the afternoon. My least productive days are those where I use all my high energy time on morning meetings, and then struggle to stay motivated during the afternoon.

If you want to make use of circadian rhythms, observe your natural energy pattern over the next few days and begin scheduling your work accordingly. Remember that it is completely normal to have some low energy times. Don't beat yourself up for being human. You can't be at the peak of energy all the time, so do the next best thing, clue-in to your high energy times and use them wisely.

Additional Energy Drains

The energy drains we have discussed thus far are the ones that occur most often and affect the broadest range of people. If you are experiencing normal fatigue, these are a good place to start looking. However, if you are experiencing abnormal fatigue (prolonged lethargy, trouble concentrating, no zest for life, enduring depression), there are some other causes you need to be aware of and discuss with your doctor.

Allergies. There are an infinite number of things people can be allergic to, from airborne particles to the foods we eat. Fatigue is often a symptom accompanying allergies.

Environmental Toxins. Your fatigue could be caused by exposure to toxins at home or at work. Radon, carbon monoxide, carbon dioxide, lead, and mercury are just a few of the harmful substances that could be the cause of fatigue.

Thyroid Problems. Improper amounts of thyroid hormone, either too little or too much, can cause fatigue.

Depression caused by a chemical imbalance. An imbalance of certain neurotransmitters has been shown to contribute to lasting depression. Sometimes this physiological problem can be remedied relatively quickly by administration of antidepressant drugs.

CFIDS (Chronic Fatigue Immune Deficiency Syndrome). A relatively new illness, CFIDS is the disease of chronic fatigue. CFIDS is hard to diagnose because its primary symptom, chronic fatigue, is also a symptom of many other diseases.

If you feel that you are abnormally fatigued don't take a chance, see your doctor. If you suspect CFIDS, make sure you see a doctor who is familiar with it. Many physicians are not trained in diagnosing fatigue related disorders, so learn as much as you can on your own so you can ask good questions. If you want to learn more, I recommend the first three books listed as references at the end of this chapter.

Whether you are experiencing normal or abnormal fatigue, stay aware of things that can drain your energy. See your doctor if you need to. For most people, removing these energy drains will create a significant boost in vitality. If you want to go beyond just removing the blockages to natural energy, to proactively boosting your energy level, read on.

Energy Boosters

The following methods and techniques can be used to bolster an already adequate energy level. If you remove energy drains and also add some of these boosters, you'll be amazed at how good you will feel.

Aerobic Exercise

Aerobic exercise is exercise done at a pace such that the body can supply oxygen to its cells on an ongoing basis. The word *aerobic* means "in the presence of oxygen." Because oxygen is supplied to muscle cells on a continuous basis, aerobic exercise can be performed continuously for long periods of time (up to several hours). Examples of aerobic exercises include: running, walking, cross country skiing, and cycling. Anaerobic exercise, meaning "without oxygen," can only be done in short spurts because the bloodstream cannot supply enough oxygen to meet the requirements of muscle fibers. Examples of anerobic exercise include wind sprints and weight lifting. Both types of exercise are highly beneficial, but it is aerobic exercise that holds the greatest promise for increasing your overall energy level. Studies have shown that aerobic exercise increases the number of red blood cells, increasing the blood's ability to carry oxygen to the rest of the body.

In addition to its physiological benefits, aerobic exercise boasts many psychological benefits as well. In one study conducted by Dr. Robert Dustman, two groups who did aerobic exercise improved "reasoning, memory, reaction time, and mental flexibility." Another study showed that a consistent routine of jogging did more to reduce depression than talking to a therapist. Aerobic exercise also enhances sleep, improves mood, and increases metabolism; there is almost no end to its benefits. But you don't need studies and research to prove the value of aerobic exercise. Just try it for yourself and you'll be convinced. Start slowly and consider some of the following as you develop your exercise routine.

> **Walking.** An exercise easy for anyone to do, walking can be the source of significant energy gains. Research by Robert Thayer of the University of California at Long Beach has shown that a brisk walk can leave you reved up for as much as two hours.

> **Jogging.** Jogging is a great overall exercise because it involves almost all the muscles in the body. It is also easy to do because it requires very little equipment. A pair of jogging shorts and running shoes are all that's required. Be careful though, start

slowly, don't run when it's very hot outside, and watch for cars if you are running on the street.

Ski Machines. A Nordic Trac or other type of ski machine is an excellent exercise because it gets all the muscles in the body working together and has a very low risk of injury. Cross-country skiing, whether done on a machine or outdoors, is deceptively challenging. It develops coordination and balance as well as cardiovascular fitness. Disadvantages are the high cost of the machine and the space required to store it.

Cycling. Similar to cross country skiing, cycling has little chance of injury from the exercise itself. You can either ride a bicycle outdoors or a stationary bicycle indoors (I guess you could ride a traditional bike indoors, but it could be kind of tough coming through the living room at 30 miles per hour.) If you choose to ride outside, always wear a helmet and beware approaching cars. Disadvantages of stationary bikes are that they can be expensive and some people find them boring.

Stair Climbers. Stair climbing has become an extremely popular exercise in recent years. Stair climbing machines combine great cardiovascular exercise with muscle toning in the legs and buttocks. Disadvantages of stair climbing machines is their high cost, space required to store them, and that they only work the lower body.

Aerobics Classes. Aerobics classes, where you get together with a group of people and follow the dance steps of the instructor, are a great source of aerobic exercise. Because you meet other people, the classes provide social interaction as well as exercise. This social interaction helps provide motivation. The recent addition of "low impact" aerobics to avoid knee and ankle injuries have made exercise classes even safer. The disadvantages of aerobics classes are that you must always travel to the gym for your workout and, because they occur at a fixed time, you can't be as flexible about when you exercise.

One question that comes up often when people are considering starting an exercise program is, "Do I buy my own equipment or go to a gym?" The answer is really based on individual preference. From a purely financial standpoint, the $300 or so dollars you'll spend for a year's membership at a gym is cheap for all the equipment you'll get to use. Instead of spending $500 or more for your own ski machine, for the price of your gym membership you'll be able to use any machine you like. Then you can purchase one if you are so inclined. Personally, I like the social interaction at the gym. One of my favorite exercises is running, which I could do easily from my home, but I often go to the gym anyway. I like the atmosphere and I find it motivating to be around other people who are dedicated to exercise. It makes me feel like I'm not alone in my quest for a healthy body.

As with any exercise program, consult your doctor before you begin. You don't have to work out incredibly hard to experience huge benefits. Start in small steps and do it often. There is nothing greater you can do for your physiological and psychological well-being than oxygenating aerobic exercise.

The Sugar Blues

The primary fuels used by the cells of your body are glucose and oxygen. If there is a deficiency of either of these, you will feel tired and have difficulty thinking clearly. Though it's difficult to have too much oxygen, blood sugar levels are a more delicate balance. Too little blood sugar and you feel wiped out, too much and you eventually develop diabetes. The body controls blood sugar by secreting the hormone insulin from the pancreas. Insulin stimulates the formation of glycogen from blood glucose, thus reducing glucose levels in the blood. When you eat something you feel a burst of energy as your blood sugar rises, but because it is dangerous for it to be too high, the pancreas secretes insulin to bring blood sugar levels back to normal. If the intake of sugar is a quick spike (as with a candy bar or any food high in sugar), the insulin will overcompensate and drop blood sugar below its normal level, leaving you feeling wiped out. This see-saw response is what's known as a "crash," or the "sugar blues." In order to compensate for blood sugar levels which are now dangerously low, your adrenal glands pour adrenaline into your blood, raising blood sugar, but making you feel nervous and jittery. Some people are more susceptible to the peaks and valleys of blood sugar than others. When a person is particularly susceptible they are called hypoglycemic. Although eating sugar when you are feeling low may make you feel better quickly, this burst of energy is usually short lived, and can bring about a crash that will make you feel even worse. Eating a candy bar when you are feeling lethargic is one of the worst things you can do to effect a lasting increase in energy.

The speed with which foods are converted into glucose is an important factor in triggering this see-saw response. As you would probably guess, refined sugar (sucrose) is very easily converted into glucose. Eating sugar, especially sugar by itself, will set in motion the see-saw response we've talked about. Surprisingly however, there are foods that are converted into glucose more quickly than refined sugar. I say surprisingly because some of these foods include things you might never associate with sugar or even sweetness; things like carrots, lima beans, and baked potatoes. These foods are even more powerful at triggering the see-saw response than eating a handful of refined white sugar.

Tests have been done in which a person's blood sugar is monitored after eating certain foods. The change in blood sugar that occurs after a food is eaten is called the glycemic response. Based on these tests, researchers have created what's called the "glycemic index," a measure of how quickly certain foods raise blood sugar. You can see the glycemic index for a selected group of foods in table 5.1. The higher the number, the more quickly the food is converted into glucose.

If you want to avoid the sugar blues, try some of the following.

Avoid foods high on the glycemic index. In table 5.1, the higher the glycemic index, the faster those foods are converted into glucose and the more likely they are to cause a blood sugar crash. Avoid the sugar blues by avoiding foods high on the glycemic index.

Reduce refined sugar in your diet (candy bars, cakes, pies, etc.). Most people consider this to be a large sacrifice. For many it is a sacrifice they are unwilling to make. If you don't want to reduce

Table 5.1 Glycemic Response of Selected Foods[3]

Food	Glycemic Index	Food	Glycemic Index
BREADS		**LEGUMES**	
white bread	100	peanuts	19
whole wheat	100	red lentils	43
sourdough rye	83	chickpeas	49
pumpernickel	80	kidney beans	51
		black beans	60
CEREALS -GRAINS		lima beans	115
barley	31	**FRUIT**	
bulgar	65		
spaghetti	66	cherries	32
rice	83	plum	34
		grapefruit	36
VEGETABLES		peach	40
		pear	47
green peas	74	apple	53
yam	74	grapes	66
corn	87	orange juice	67
carrots	133	orange	67
potato		banana	79
boiled	81	raisins	93
instant	116		
baked	135	**DAIRY**	
		milk	49
SUGAR		ice cream	52
sucrose (table sugar)	86	yogurt	52

---

[3] Adapted from *The American Journal of Clinical Nutrition*, October 1985, Volume 46, page 606.

sugar all the time, try moderating your sugar intake Monday through Friday. This will give you more energy during the work week and, because you can still eat sugar on the weekends, you won't feel totally deprived of the foods you love.

Emphasize proteins and complex carbohydrates (chicken, fish, bread, pasta) with a low glycemic index in your diet. These are converted into blood sugar more slowly and therefore produce a more constant blood sugar level.

Eat more small meals during the day rather than fewer large ones. After eating a balanced meal, you have a steady conversion of food into glucose for about four hours. By eating three light meals and 2-3 healthy snacks, you can maintain a consistent blood sugar level (your ultimate goal) throughout the day.

Consider using chromium as a supplement. Many experts believe that chromium helps the body moderate blood sugar levels. Any health and nutrition store will carry chromium supplements.

Relaxation

We all need a safe haven where we can relax and insulate ourselves from the stresses of life. For some this safe haven might take the form of lying on the beach. For others it might be gardening or playing a round of golf, and for still others sitting in a quiet place meditating. Whatever form it takes, the purpose of relaxation is to protect us from the dangerous effects of prolonged stress.

When you endure ongoing stress with no reprieve, you become irritable, don't think as clearly, and eventually loose your zest and passion for your work. We call this loss of zest "burnout," and it can only be avoided by regularly taking time to separate yourself from the stress that causes it.

Several years ago I had the opportunity to hear Olympic gold medalist Dan Jansen describe his experience in training for his four trips to the Olympic games. He said that for Olympic athletes *everything* is training. World-class athletes view every aspect of their life as preparation for optimal performance, from exercise, to what they eat, to getting enough sleep, to making sure they have enough time to relax.

Jansen said as he trained for the '92 games, "even playing a round of golf was part of training because an athlete has to balance relaxation with the stress of training to create optimal performance."

In his landmark book, *The Relaxation Response*, Dr. Herbert Bensen describes the physiological changes associated with going from a stressed state to a state of deep relaxation: heart rate slows, blood pressure decreases, and breathing softens. He also proved that if this relaxation response is triggered often enough, it will cause us to experience these physiological changes even when we aren't practicing meditation or some other form of relaxation. This overall reduction of blood pressure, heart rate, and the other physiological symptoms of stress has significant benefits to health and longevity. The point is, there is a very sound *physiological reason*, backed up by scientific data, for us to make time to relax.

Deep relaxation comes from tuning out the external world by focusing intently on one thing. You often experience this type of relaxation when you become totally absorbed in a pleasurable task: golf, gardening, or even going to the movies. During the time you are absorbed in the task, you aren't even aware the world around you exists. You may have experienced this from time to time when you're driving a familiar route and you become so focused on one thought that you arrive at your destination with no memory of the trip. When that type of absorption happens, you experience a significant reduction in the physiological symptoms associated with stress. The reduction of these stress symptoms is what Bensen calls the "relaxation response." And it is this response that protects us from the ill effects of prolonged stress.

Bensen did much work to show how this relaxation response can be triggered through meditation. Here meditation has no religious significance. It is simply defined as a quieting of the mind. To trigger the relaxation response, find a quiet, comfortable environment where you won't be disturbed for an hour or so. Begin by closing your eyes and taking several slow, deep breaths. Feel all your muscles relaxing and try to put any thoughts and cares of the day out of your mind. As you sit quietly, begin to repeat a mantra, or single word, over and over.

Buddhists use the sound a-a-u-m, a-a-u-m, a-a-u-m. You can use any sound or word you like. Some teachers of meditation recommend using the word "one." The purpose of the mantra is to keep extraneous thoughts from creeping into your mind. The goal is to be completely calm, quiet, and serene. The rhythm and pace of sound vibrations created by repeating the mantra aloud also help trigger a state of deep relaxation. Plan on taking as much as 30-60 minutes to do these sessions in the beginning. At first you will probably have some difficulty triggering the relaxation response, but keep up the meditation practice. When you reach a state of deep relaxation you'll know it. You'll emerge refreshed and with a new sense of vibrancy and energy.

Relaxation is an important part of preparing for peak performance. World class athletes have know this for years. For your own relaxation, try some of the following:

> **Take a vacation.** For most of us it takes 4-5 days to really forget the cares of our jobs and lives and fully relax. Take a vacation of at least a full week no less than once a year.
>
> **Leave work at work.** Don't bring work home, either in your briefcase or in your mind. The world's most successful people have time for their personal lives, so should you. You'll be more effective by having some time away from your work than you will by thinking about it constantly.
>
> **Meditate.** Use the process outlined here and begin practicing meditation. With experience you'll be able to trigger the relaxation response in as little as five minutes.
>
> **Create "sanctuary time."** Sanctuary time is sacred time in which you refuse to do any work or even think about work. It is time just for you. I designate part of Saturday and the entire day on Sunday as my sanctuary time. If I can't get my work done Monday through Friday (including a little time Saturday morning for reading) then it just doesn't get done.
>
> **Do things you like doing.** Make a list of activities you find pleasurable and relaxing and make time to do them. Don't feel

guilty for taking time to relax. As Dan Jansen said, relaxation is a legitimate part of creating optimal performance.

Caffeine

Caffeine. Some people use none at all and live lives of abundant energy. Others couldn't survive a day without it. It is probably the most prevalent drug used in the United States, but should it be? Several important questions need to be answered for you to make an informed decision about whether caffeine should be part of your energy management program:

- What are the physiological effects of caffeine that provide the energy bursts we've all experienced?
- What do doctors and other experts recommend with regard to using caffeine?
- If you choose to use it, what is the optimal amount?

Caffeine works by stimulating the adrenal glands. Adrenaline is the hormone that is secreted when we are in a "fight or flight" situation. It causes increased heart rate, blood pressure, and blood flow to the skeletal muscles. It makes your senses finely tuned and ready for action, but if you are not in a fight or a flight situation, adrenaline will leave you feeling edgy and jittery. That's why you feel shaky when you drink too much coffee. When caffeine is no longer entering the bloodstream, adrenal function slows and you experience a "drop off," or caffeine induced tiredness.

Many health enthusiasts believe they are better off with no caffeine at all. However, most experts agree that a little caffeine can be beneficial. It stimulates you without any adverse side-effects. I have tried both approaches. I have used small amounts of caffeine in the morning, and I once went for almost two years with none at all. During the time I was not using caffeine, I did enjoy some benefits. I never felt the caffeine jitters and had a smoother more relaxed energy throughout the day. But there were also mornings where I was significantly less productive that I would have been with a little caffeine. I currently use a *small* amount in the morning and feel that I am more productive overall than without it.

Just what is a "small amount" of caffeine? A study conducted at the Massachusetts Institute of Technology reports that the most effective dose is 128 milligrams, approximately the amount you would get in two cups of coffee. A dose higher than that didn't increase the alertness of subjects in the study. Of course the optimal amount will vary depending on body weight, metabolism, and other variables, but it's clear that 10 cups of coffee is too much.

The amount of caffeine in beverages can vary widely, but here are some ranges:

coffee	30-175 mg per cup
tea	10-100 mg per cup
soda	40-50 mg per 12 ounce can

The bottom-line is this, whether you use caffeine or not is a decision you will have to make for yourself. If you choose to eliminate all caffeine you'll probably feel a little more relaxed, but you may have some days where your productivity suffers. Many experts agree that in *small doses* caffeine is helpful. Just be careful not to use too much.

Power Breathing

Throughout this chapter we've emphasized the two primary ingredients for energy: fuel (glucose) and oxygen. Anything you can do to ensure you are getting optimal amounts of these two ingredients is important to producing maximum energy. Blood circulates through the lungs and picks up oxygen molecules by attaching them to red blood cells. Having the blood fully oxygenated when it leaves the lungs is obviously better than having it partially oxygenated. That's the purpose of power breathing.

If you want a quick energy boost, try this power breathing exercise. Go through several cycles of these three steps to increase the oxygen in your blood and therefore your vitality.

1. **Breathe from the diaphragm.** When you are breathing from your diaphragm, you should see your stomach move in and out more than you see your chest rise and fall. Breathe in through the nose, out through the mouth.

2. **Hold the air in your lungs for a few seconds.** Try breathing in to the count of four and holding for a count of eight.

3. **Exhale fully.** Remove as much air from your lungs as possible by pushing with your diaphragm.

In addition to fully oxygenating the blood, power breathing stimulates the lymph system, helping to carry waste products away from the cells and out of the body. You can use power breathing any time you're feeling a little pooped, or even when you're feeling great, to keep you going.

Dietary Supplements

Dietary supplements are substances used to supplement the nutritional value you get from your diet. Many supplements are rumored to possess magical powers for creating vitality. I've not experienced these magical powers personally, though I have experienced mildly beneficial effects from some of them. If you are thinking about using supplements as part of your energy management program, you will want to consider some of the following.

Vitamin and Mineral Supplements. Though medical opinion varies widely on the need for vitamin and mineral supplements, most doctors agree that deficiencies of needed vitamins and minerals can cause fatigue. There are those who believe in megavitamins (as much as 100 times the recommended daily allowance), while others contend that you can get all the nutrition you need from a balanced diet. You can take a blood test to determine blood levels of vitamins and minerals, but it will not tell you for sure if you are getting enough. In his book, *Doctor, Why am I so Tired?*, Dr. Richard Podell recommends a daily multivitamin for those who suspect their diets are not providing needed nutrients. In most cases a multivitamin is completely safe, and some people have noticed significant gains in energy just from this supplement.

Choline. Choline is thought to be a building block for the neurotransmitter acetylcholine and has been shown to enhance alertness in some people. It is found in some forms of fish, one of the reasons fish is sometimes referred to as "brain food." I have personally used choline supplements with noticeable results.

Ginseng. Ginseng has been proven to increase the ability of blood to carry oxygen. An extract from the ginseng plant, it was first used in the Orient. You will find many varieties on the shelves of health food stores, including Siberian Ginseng. Siberian Ginseng is an extract that does not actually come from the ginseng plant, but does have energy improving properties.

Dimethelglycine (DMG). DMG (or vitamin B15) has also been shown to increase the ability of blood to carry oxygen. It gained much popularity in the 1960's when Russian athletes used it to enhance their performance in the Olympics.

L-carnitine. L-carnitine is an amino acid which helps provide fuel to the mitochondria. It has been shown to increase oxygen usage and aid in burning fat for energy.

Wheat Germ (Octacosanol). Athletes have known of the benefits of wheat germ for years. The active ingredient in wheat germ is a substance called octacosanol. Testing has proven it's ability to increase strength, stamina, and cardiovascular function.

All these supplements can be found on the shelves of any well stocked health and nutrition store. I don't recommend using them all. Try one at a time, take it in its recommended dosage, and observe the effects it has on your energy.

In this chapter we've covered a number of techniques for managing a critical driver of sales activity, physical energy. We've discussed things that drain your energy, and I've given you ideas for how to boost your energy. Even if you are already a high energy person, you should be able to benefit from at least a few of the ideas presented here. If, like me, you sometimes experience less than optimal energy levels, this could easily be the most important chapter in this book. Experiment with the things we've talked about and see what works for you. Be sure to use good judgement, and if you feel you have abnormal fatigue, see your doctor.

I made this the first chapter on "Creating Activity" because without physical energy the techniques that follow will not be nearly as effective. In chapter 6 we will move from a focus on the physical to a focus on the mental side of activity management.

Q&A:

Q: How do I know if I have an energy problem?

A: "Problem" is a strong word. Almost all of us have an energy deficiency from time to time. If you don't have the energy to do all the things you want to do (work hard at your job, take care of the house, enjoy time with your family) I would call that a problem. If you consistently have difficulty getting out of bed, or feel yourself losing energy during the work day, that's a problem. The effects of a lack of energy are very deceptive. You may not realize your disinterest in doing paperwork, or your reluctance to make cold calls, is primarily due to a lack of physical energy. I have a hard time defining who has a "problem" and who doesn't. Perhaps a better question would be, "Is it important for me to focus on improving my energy?" To that I can answer an emphatic yes. Everything functions better with energy. We should all be working to have more.

Q: Can you have too much energy?

A: I don't believe you can. If you're hyper and nervous from ingesting too much sugar and caffeine, of course that's not good, but I wouldn't call that energy. Remember, our definition of energy is "the ability to think, react, and perform." We can never have too much of that. It might be bad if someone could not sleep because they were too wired, but this is not the problem most people have. Of the kind of energy we're talking about; a slow, even, productive energy, you can never have too much.

Q: How soon will I see results from these techniques? How much improvement can I expect?

A: We would have to talk about specific techniques to give a specific answer, but generally from 2 days to 3 weeks. If you haven't seen some benefit in 3 weeks, the technique probably isn't working for you and you should move on to something else. Improvements can range from small to dramatic. If you've had a major energy drain: lack of sleep, poor diet, or depression, improvements could be significant. If you're not experiencing a major problem, results will probably be less dramatic.

Application Exercises

1. Go to bed an hour earlier than your normal bedtime and see if you wake feeling more refreshed.

2. Eliminate concentrated sugar (candy bars, chocolate, cookies, etc.) from your diet for a week. Although you will probably experience some cravings for sweets, you should begin to feel more energetic by the end of the week. If you like this new, more relaxed energy, keep up the practice of leaving concentrated sugar out of your diet.

3. If you don't currently have an exercise program, start one. Begin slowly, perhaps with several long walks a week. As you build up your stamina move into some of the aerobic exercises outlined in this chapter.

4. Stop by your local health food store and buy one of the supplements recommended. Try it for three weeks and see if it makes a difference. If you like the effects, keep it as part of your energy management program.

References

Ronald L. Hoffman, *Tired All The Time: How to Regain Your Lost Energy*, (New York: Poseidon Press, 1993).

David S. Bell, *Curing Fatigue: A Step-by-Step Plan to Uncover and Eliminate the Causes of Chronic Fatigue*, (Emmaus, PA: Rodale Press, 1993).

Richard N. Podell, *Doctor, Why Am I So Tired?* (New York: Pharos Books, 1987.)

Covert Bailey, *The New Fit or Fat*, (Boston: Houghton Mifflin Company, 1991.)

Herbert Benson, *The Relaxation Response*, (New York: Avon Books, 1975.)

Harvey and Marilyn Diamond, *Fit for Life*, (New York: Warner Books, 1985.)

Daniel Hammer and Barbara Barr, *Peak Energy*, (New York: G.P. Butnam's Sons, 1988.)

Judith J. Wurtman, *Managing Your Mind and Mood Through Food*, (New York: Harper & Row, 1986).

Joan Borysenko, *Minding the Body, Mending the Mind*, (Lecture in Bridgeport, CT April 1992).

Barbara H. Levine, *Your Body Believes Every Word You Say*, (Boulder, CO: Aslan Publishing, 1991).

Jennifer Rapaport, "10 Ways to Up Your Energy," *Mademoiselle*, March 1994, vol. 100, page 78.

"36 Ways to Get More Energy," *Glamor*, March 1994, vol. 92, page 208.

Daryn Eller, "Cure Your Energy Crisis," *Redbook*, July 1993, vol. 181, page 69.

"Low glycemic index carbohydrate foods in the management of hyperlipidemia," *The American Journal of Clinical Nutrition*, October 1985, vol. 42, page 606.

Chapter 6
Mental Imaging

"The predecessor to every action is a thought."

-- Emerson

Sometime in the early part of my speaking career, I was having lunch with an experience speaker who was coaching me. I was talking about how difficult it was getting started, and how I was frustrated by being asked to do presentations that weren't really on the subjects I loved most. He asked me what seemed like an infinitely reasonable question, "What subjects do you love the most?" I was taken back by his question. It's one thing to complain about how things are. It's something else altogether to describe the way you want them to be. I couldn't answer him. I knew the subjects I was currently speaking about weren't in total alignment with my passion, but I didn't know exactly what that passion was.

His question forced me to admit to myself that I didn't have a clear idea of what I wanted. As I pondered his question, I was struck with the realization that if I didn't know what I wanted, I had no right to ever expect it to happen. Even if I stumbled upon it, I might miss it, because I didn't know what "it" was. In his book, *The Psychology of Self-Esteem*, famed psychologist Nathaniel Branden says,

> "It is astonishing how few [people] ever ask themselves the question, 'What is it that I want?'"

And he goes on to say, "This is perhaps the most important question any human being can ever ask."

You can never create something in the external world until you have created it in your mind first. None of man's great achievements: skyscrapers, bridges, symphonies, or paintings were produced by a random flow of events. Someone first thought about each of those things, and then acted to bring them into existence.

Fundamental Truth #1

> Any result you have ever created began by your first thinking about it.

The Magical Power of Visualization

Everyone in sales has heard, too many times, of the great powers of visualization. Numerous authors and speakers have said something to the effect, "If you want to have a BMW, cut out a picture of a BMW and post it on your bathroom mirror. Look at it every day and think about having a BMW. Feel the BMW. Become one with the BMW. By visualizing it you will *attract it into your life.*"

Well, I've tried this approach, and all I ever got was a yellowed picture of a BMW. I don't mean to ridicule the technique. I believe keeping before you an image of what you want does have power, but only as a reminder and simple motivator. I haven't personally experienced the magical, creative power this technique is rumored to possess. *However*, I have discovered a similar technique that does possess such power.

The next sentence is extremely important. Please read it carefully. **You cannot create a behavior, act in a desired manner, or *do* anything without first creating that *behavior* in your mind.** Even behaviors that have become automatic (brushing your teeth, buttoning your shirt, combing your hair) were at one point thought about. All behavior is preceded by thought, even though in some cases that thought is exceedingly brief.

The "mental imaging" we will talk about in this chapter is DIFFERENT from what you are used to. It's different because of its application to behavior instead of results. If you want to experience true, magical, creative power, apply the same "think it first" idea that built bridges and skyscrapers to the fundamental building block of all success: your behavior. One of the most powerful, and misunderstood, techniques for behavioral modification is positive imaging of desired *behavior*.

Fundamental Truth #2

> Any *behavior* you have ever created began by your first thinking about it.

Why the Emphasis on Behavior?

Why the big focus on behavior? Because imaging behavior does seem to magically create behaviors that were previously difficult or impossible. How does imaging *behavior* do this? The answer to that question is somewhat involved and requires an understanding of precisely what's happening inside the mind in the instant just before you begin a new behavior. In the discussion that follows I will use making phone calls as an example, but the concepts can be generalized to any behavior.

Suppose on a particular morning you come into the office, have a cup of coffee, chat for a few minutes with a colleague, have a brief conversation with the secretary, and then walk back to your office. You know that it's now time to start dialing. We could say that when it's time to make calls we have "arrived" at the task of making calls. The relative level of your desire to make calls (because you want to do a good job and make money) and your desire not to make calls (caused by fear and perceived discomfort) is called "arrival position." Arrival position is your emotional attitude toward the task in the moment you are suppose to begin. If your desire to act exceeds your desire not to, you will pick up the phone and get to work. If not, you will have to change the way you are thinking about the task, or else you will turn away form the task and do something else (a process called procrastination).

So there you sit, in your office, you've had your coffee, talked with a colleague and the secretary, and now it's time to make phone calls. I'm sure there have been days when you picked up the phone and went right to work, and other days when you found something else to do. What's the difference? What happened inside your head that made you pick up the phone on one day and not on the next? In order to answer that question we have to understand a unit of behavior called a TOTE.[1]

The acronym TOTE stands for Test-Operate-Test-Exit, and is a model used to describe a small sequence of behavior. A generic TOTE model is shown in figure 6.1.

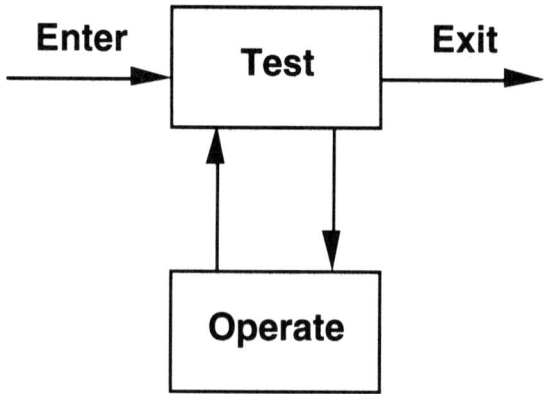

Figure 6.1: Generic TOTE

---

[1] Robert Dilts, et. al. *Neuro-Linguistic Programming: Volume 1*, (Cupertino, CA: Meta Publications, 1980), pages 28-29.

Mental Imaging • 83

A behavior that is readily modeled by a TOTE is adjusting the volume on your stereo. When you decide to listen to music and turn on the stereo, you enter the TOTE. The initial test is made when you hear the music and decide whether it is at the right volume. If it is, then the test is passed, no operation is required, and you exit the TOTE. If the music is too soft or too loud, the initial test is failed, and some operation (turning the volume knob) is necessary to satisfy the test. The knob is turned and the volume tested, turned, tested, turned, tested, etc. until a satisfactory level is reached. When a satisfactory level is reached, the test is passed, and the behavior sequence is exited. Keep in mind, all these things happen extremely quickly, and almost always below the threshold of consciousness.

    Now let's use the model to analyze that instant just before you pick up the phone. When you sit down at your desk, having just completed some behavior sequence, it is now time to create a new one. Knowing it is time to make calls, you are entering a *decision* TOTE for making calls. For most people, the initial test consists of creating an image of themselves making calls, then testing how that image makes them "feel." If it feels right (i.e. creates neutral to positive emotions), the test is passed and they exit the decision TOTE and begin making calls. If however the image doesn't feel right (i.e. creates negative emotions) the test is failed and some operation must be performed before they pass the test and exit the TOTE. The operation takes the form of imaging alternate behaviors (doing paperwork, going to the bathroom, getting a cup of coffee, etc.), or alternate versions of the original behavior. The new image is tested, and if it passes the test (feels right) the TOTE is exited and they begin *that* behavior. Figure 6.2 shows a decision TOTE for making phone calls.

    From the TOTE model it becomes fairly obvious that if we would like to make calls more consistently, we want the image of phone calls to generate positive emotions and therefore pass the test. We can ensure this by pre-conditioning the emotions associated with making calls. This is what we are doing during mental rehearsal. By consciously

84 • Activity-Based Selling

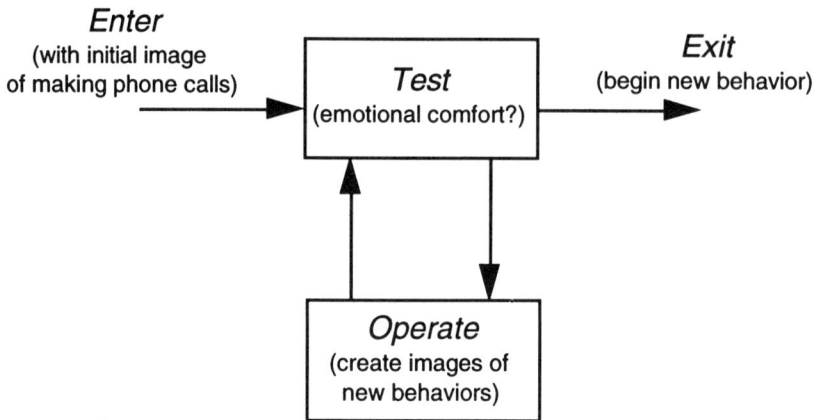

Figure 6.2: Decision TOTE for Phone Calls

seeing yourself making calls and experiencing positive emotions, you are connecting those emotions with that behavior. *The more vivid the image and the stronger the emotions, the greater the association.* For this reason we will strive for vivid images and strong positive emotions during mental rehearsal of desired behaviors. Done properly, mental rehearsal will help you consistently pass through the decision TOTE and into the task you had previously avoided (i.e. it will reduce your task reluctance for making phone calls).

The Five Senses: Building Blocks of Powerful Mental Images

Before we talk about using mental imaging as a tool for managing sales activity, it's important to understand the basic elements, or building blocks, that make up effective images. Mental imaging is more than just visualization. The word "image" refers to a mental representation involving all five senses.

Everything you have ever experienced has come to you through your five senses (sight, sound, touch or "feeling," taste, and smell). All the memories stored in you subconscious are built from these five senses. Each of these senses has a number of qualities that define it further. Some of the qualities associated with the three major senses are listed in table 6.1.

Making your imagined experience as vivid as possible will increase the strength of the imprint and thereby increase the impact of your mental rehearsal. Our senses, along with their associated qualities, are the building blocks used to create these vivid images. Creating a vivid image requires paying careful attention to the qualities

Table 6.1 The Three Major Senses and Their Associated Qualities

Seeing:	*Hearing:*	*Feeling:*
brightness	volume	texture
nearness	pitch	temperature
color or black & white	tempo	soft or hard
movement	pauses	pressure
angle of view	direction	proximity

as well as the senses that make up the image. Relax as you read the following example and experience the power using all your senses to create a strong, vivid image.

The Beach Scene

You are walking along the beach. It's mid-July; very, very *hot*; five o'clock in the afternoon. The sun is getting low on the horizon although it has not yet begun to set. The sky is a brilliant *blue*, the sun a blazing *yellow*. Feel the *heat* from the sun against your face; feel the *warmth* of its rays against your skin.

You are barefoot. Feel the *hot, dry* sand beneath your feet. Walk closer to the water. Feel the *wet, cold*, firmly packed sand beneath your feet.

Hear the beating of the waves, the rhythmic crashing, back and forth, to and fro, of the water against the sand. Hear the *loud, high* cries of the gulls circling overhead. You continue walking.

Suddenly you come to a sand dune, a mound of *white* sand covered with deep *pink* moss roses, bright *yellow* buttercups. You sit down on that mound of sand. You look out to sea. The sea is like a mirror of *silver* reflecting the sun's rays, a mass of pure, *white* light.

You are gazing fixedly into that light. As you continue to stare at the sun's reflection off the water, you begin to see dots of *purple*, darting flecks of violet. There's a violet line along the horizon, a *purple* halo around the flowers; everywhere *purple* and *silver*.

Now the sun is beginning to set. With each motion, with each movement of the sun into the sea, you go deeper and deeper relaxed ... and when the sun has sunk into the ocean, you will be in a profound state of relaxation.

The sky is turning *red, crimson, scarlet, gold, amber,* as the sun sets. You are engulfed in a deep *purple* twilight, a velvety *blue* haze. You look up at the night sky. It's clear, filled with stars ... a brilliant starry night ... the *soft, low* roar of the waves, the taste and smell of the *salt*, the sea, the sky, and you ... And you feel yourself carried upward and outward into space, one with the universe.[2]

If you're like most people, the focus on color, brightness, temperature, and texture create an extremely vivid and realistic experience of the beach, one you'll remember for many weeks. Let's try one more example.

---

[2] Reprinted with the permission of Simon & Schuster from *Creative Imagery* by William Fezler. Copyright © 1989 by Dr. William Fezler.

Fresh Lemons

Picture in front of you a large bowl of lemons. They are perfectly ripe, *juicy, cold*, just from the refrigerator. The *moisture* from condensation runs down and along the *pebbly* skin of one of the *bright, yellow* lemons. With a very *sharp* knife you cut one of the lemons in half. You can immediately smell the *aroma* of *citrus*. The inside is *firm, glistening, yellow*, with eight perfect triangles and two small seeds. You pick up half of the lemon, move it close to you nose and smell. You stick you tongue out and lick the cut surface. With your tongue you feel the *texture* of the meat, the divisions, and the seeds. The sensations of *cold* and *sour* simultaneously bombard your senses. Finally you open your mouth wide and bite down *firmly* on the lemon. Your bottom teeth on the outer, *pebbly* skin, your top teeth break into the freshly cut surface and spray you mouth with *cold, fresh, sour*, juice.

One of our bodily functions under the control of the subconscious is salivation. If you experienced an increase in saliva while reading the last paragraph, you have proven that your subconscious cannot distinguish between a real experience and one that is vividly imagined. By creating vivid images you are constructing memories that are every bit as strong as memories of actual experiences. This is the power of the five senses. By focusing them, you can create positive images of desired behaviors, allowing you to flow effortlessly through the TOTE and avoid the task reluctance so damaging to personal motivation. The more vivid the image, the more powerful the behavior modification.

Creating Sales Activity

All this discussion about TOTEs, senses, qualities, and vivid images leaves one question unanswered: How do you use this stuff to increase sales activity? What follows is a step-by-step process for using mental rehearsal to modify behavior and create effective sales activity.

Step 1: *Identify Desired Behavior*

Identify a specific sales behavior as the subject of your mental rehearsal. It could be something where you want to reduce your tendency to procrastinate, increase your consistency, or where you just need a little added motivation. A good place to start is one of your key sales activities identified in chapter 4.

Step 2: *Define Next Opportunity*

Decide when and where the next opportunity for the behavior will occur. Later today in your office? Tomorrow morning during a sales call? Some other time? When you do your mental rehearsal, imagine yourself in the same time and place as your next opportunity.

Step 3: *Rehearse Mentally*

Find a quiet place where you can concentrate undisturbed for at least five minutes. Take several slow deep breaths in and out. Feel yourself relaxing more as you exhale each breath. Close your eyes and imagine yourself in your desired activity. Not only *in* the activity, but *enjoying* the activity and producing the *results* you want. Imagine yourself tomorrow morning, at your desk, phone in hand, speaking to a prospect, smiling, enjoying the process, and closing the sale. Now fine tune your senses and their associated qualities to make the experience as real as possible. See yourself in color, move in closer, make the picture brighter. Hear the voice of the prospect on the phone in a very soothing, pleasing tone. Feel the internal satisfaction you get when the prospect says yes. Focus on that feeling for 2-3 seconds. Cycle back through the imagined scene several times. Feel the excitement and pleasure you can experience while making phone calls.

The power of mental rehearsal comes from making a strong subconscious connection between a very satisfying feeling and your desired behavior. Once this connection is made, you'll be surprised at how much easier and more enjoyable the activity will be.

Mental imaging is the process of consciously creating mental pictures of your desired goal or outcome. The technique is typically taught as a process for creating results-oriented goals, but its effectiveness in this application is hard to measure. The more powerful application of mental imaging is that of *behavioral* modification, where you imagine yourself executing a desired behavior shortly before your next opportunity to execute that behavior. The instant just before you do or do not begin this behavior is critical. By using mental imaging to associate positive emotions with the behavior, you reduce the subconscious tendency to imagine alternate behaviors and potentially procrastinate. The more vivid your image of the desired behavior, and the stronger the positive emotions generated by it, the more effective your mental rehearsal will be.

In this chapter we've focused on managing your emotional response to the thought of certain activities. We've done this because emotions have a tremendous impact on productivity. But sometimes we experience powerful negative emotions that have nothing to do with our images of future activities. These more general negative emotions have an even greater power in reducing sales activity because they pervade everything we do. It is these more general negative feelings that are the subject of the next chapter.

Q&A:

The following are answers to some of the most frequently asked questions about mental rehearsal:

Q: What is the best time to practice mental rehearsal?

A: The time that works best for you. It could be in the morning before work, at different points throughout the day, or in the evening. I prefer the evening before when I am planning the behavior for the next day. By doing my mental rehearsal at night, I am further removed from the actual experience and feel freer to imagine how good it will feel when I do it. I also find that there is some benefit to letting my subconscious work on the image over night.

Q: How much time will this take?

A: *Very* little. One of the greatest benefits of this technique is that it can be done in a very short period of time. My sessions usually take two minutes or less. Remember, the purpose is to create a strong connection between positive emotions and the image of the behavior. As your skill at creating vivid images and strong emotions increases, you'll find that the time you need to spend is even shorter. I've experienced significant results from as little as five seconds of mental rehearsal.

Q: How long will I have to practice before I see results?

A: You should see results immediately. By immediately, I mean that if you imagine a desired behavior the night before, you should notice a significant reduction in your tendency to avoid the task the next day.

Q: Will I really learn to *enjoy* making cold calls?

A: Maybe. Our goal is to ease activity. Even with mental rehearsal, making cold calls will still require some effort. If you rated your hatred for making cold calls on a scale from 1-10 at a 10+, mental rehearsal probably won't make you love cold calls. But it may very well reduce your dislike from a level 10 to a level 6 or even a 5. And that has significant value.

Q: Is there any way I can do this wrong?

A: Not really. There's no way you will hurt yourself through positive imaging. The only thing you could do "wrong" is to not create strong emotions and vivid images. Remember to see yourself *doing* the activity. See phone calls being made, papers being filed, letters being mailed. *Feel* the satisfaction of doing the tasks, then see them completed and done, and amplify the great feeling this completion gives you.

Application Exercises:

1. Choose an important sales activity that you will have the opportunity to perform tomorrow. Take two minutes sometime this evening and imagine yourself successfully exhibiting the behavior. See yourself enjoying the experience and achieving outstanding results.

2. The next time you find yourself procrastinating, delaying, or avoiding an important task, stop and take conscious control of the images in your head. If you want to successfully exit the TOTE you are in, create an image that generates positive emotions. Immediately after this visualization exercise, dive in and begin the task.

3. Practice using all your senses and their associated qualities whenever you are imagining anything (i.e. while reading a book, daydreaming about your next vacation, or thinking about a meeting with a prospect).

Suggested Reading:

Shakti Gawain, *Creative Visualization*, (New York: Bantam Books, 1978.)

Maxwell Maltz, *Psycho-Cybernetics*, (New York, Prentice-Hall, 1960.)

William Fezler, *Creative Imagery: How to Visualize in All Five Senses*, (New York: Simon & Schuster, 1989.)

Chapter 7
Managing Negative Emotions

Salesperson: "Well, that's true, but last week we agreed..."
Prospect (interrupting): "I'm sorry. I'm really busy. Could we do this later?"
Salesperson: (surprised) "Uhhh-oooo-kay, sure ... uh, why don't I give you a call this afternoon. What's a good time for you?"
Prospect: "Well ... there isn't really any good time. (pause) Listen, I'm sorry you've done so much work on this, but we're not interested at this time."
Salesperson (with *great* surprise): "Not interested!?! But last week you said ... "
Prospect (interrupting): "I know what I said, but things have changed. We're not interested anymore ... (to secretary) Yes, tell him I'll be right there ... Again, I'm sorry. Thanks for all your work. Good luck. I've really got to go now. Goodbye. (click)"

Disappointment. Frustration. Anger. What emotions would you experience after a conversation like that? Would those feelings encourage you to make more or fewer calls that day? Would your calls be more or less effective because of those emotions?

Triggers for negative emotions are omnipresent in the life of a salesperson. And the level and effectiveness of your activity depends greatly on whether you manage these negative emotions or allow them to manage you.

Key Premise:

> *If you experience negative emotions during the time you should be creating activity, it will reduce the level and effectiveness of that activity.*

We all experience negative emotions from time to time. We always will. It's a natural part of the ebb and flow of life. These emotions become a problem only when they block needed action or keep you in a prolonged state of depression or pain. How you handle negative emotions not only affects the volume of activity you produce, but ultimately determines whether sales is a career you pursue with passion or a job you simply endure.

Emotions, What Are They?

If asked, could you give a clear and concise definition for the word *emotion*? It's easy to get so comfortable with common words that we never explore what they really mean.

> *"For what are emotions? Who is able to easily and briefly explain them? ... Surely we understand well enough when we speak of them. What then are emotions? If nobody asks me I know; but if I were desirous to explain it to someone - plainly I know not."*[1]

Emotions aren't as easily defined as you might initially think. The internal experience one person labels as anger could be significantly

---

[1] Adapted from a quote by Saint Augustine.

different from the experience someone else calls anger. And the range and combination of emotions is virtually unlimited. There are over 500 words in the English language describing emotions. After doing extensive research, it became obvious to me that there is no clear agreement on the exact nature of emotions. Still, if we are serious about managing them, it would be valuable to put a framework around what we do know. Let me see if I can summarize it.

An emotion is *an internal reaction to an external event*. Someone scratches your new car and you become *angry*. Someone rejects you and you feel *hurt*. The stock market takes a tumble and you feel *anxious*. Something happens "out there," in the environment, and it triggers something "in here," inside of you. That something inside of you is what we call an emotion.

One thing we do know is that emotions are made up of discrete physical and psychological components. The physical components of anger can include: increased heart rate, deeper and more rapid breathing, and increased perspiration. Psychological components include: changes in the internal images we see, changes in our internal dialogue, and changes in how we "feel."

To a large extent "feelings," or visceral sensations, are the component we most associate with emotions. Tactile sensations are acquired with the outside of the body. Move your finger over sandpaper and you sense "roughness"; over glass and you feel "smoothness." Press your cheek to the refrigerator door and feel "coolness." Visceral sensations originate *inside* the body. The word visceral comes from the word *viscus*, meaning "an internal organ of the body." A visceral feeling is something you feel in your internal organs. When you say, "I have a twisting in my gut," you may be speaking more literally than you think. An event triggers a flexing of the muscles surrounding your stomach and that is what you *feel*. Emotions usually, if not always, have a visceral component.

Psychologists generally agree that there are two dimensions to all emotions: *hedonic tone* and *arousal*. Hedonic tone is the pleasant-unpleasant dimension. Arousal is the excitement-calm dimension.

96 • Activity-Based Selling

Figure 7.1 gives examples of various emotions in the tone-arousal model. Anger is an unpleasant emotion with excessive excitement. Depression is an unpleasant emotion with excessive calm.

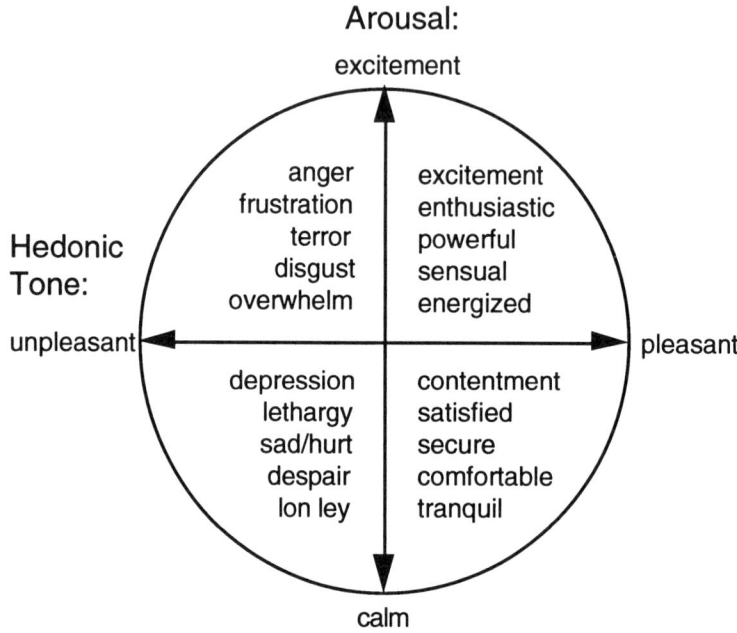

Figure 7.1: Hedonic Tone and Arousal

Emotions with low arousal (depression, anxiety, etc.) tend to last longer than those with high arousal. Depression could last for days or weeks while anger or excitement are usually much shorter.

What Causes Emotions?

We've already said that outside events cause emotions. But how specifically does an event *cause* an emotion? What is the process that turns a scratch on the door of your new car into the emotion we call anger? Listed below are three generally agreed upon causes that will be important for understanding the techniques that follow. Although this is not a comprehensive list, it should shed some light on 90% of the emotions experienced by the typical salesperson.

Cause #1: *Conditioned Responses*

Ivan Pavlov won the Nobel prize in 1904 for his work on digestion. During his research, Pavlov noticed that not only did his dogs salivate when food was introduced into their mouths, but also at the sight of food, or even the sound of the footsteps of their food handler. Intrigued, Pavlov began to study this phenomenon in and of itself. He found that when the same stimulus was regularly paired with a given response, soon the stimulus could be used to trigger the response. His work formed the basis for what we know today as classical conditioning.

A handshake is an example of a conditioned response. When you meet a new person and they reach out their hand, you *automatically* move your hand to meet theirs. Without thinking, you simply respond. You have responded in the same way so many times you don't even think about it any more. It has become a "conditioned" response. If it's true that we have automatic physical responses, doesn't it also makes sense that we could have automatic emotional responses? The following excerpt indicates that conditioned emotional responses are not only possible, but very common.

> "It appears that emotional responses are particularly susceptible to this sort of conditioning. Emotional reactions such as fear, anger, and disgust involve heightened activity of organs and glands controlled by the autonomic nervous system (e.g., the heart and the respiratory and digestive systems). Reactions of these organ systems, and the emotions that accompany them, *are readily learned through classical conditioning.*"[2]

---

[2] Richard M. Lerner, et. al., *Psychology*, (New York: MacMillan Publishing Company, 1986), page 184.

John is an experienced salesperson working for a software development company. When John was a child, his mother was very strict. She believed that children should be seen and not heard. When John would talk a lot or make a play for his mother's attention, she would say, "John, I'm not interested in hearing that right now," or "John, I'm not interested in this," or simply, "I'm not interested." On one occasion, when some of his mother's friends were visiting, John accidentally slammed his finger in the door. He ran to his mother for comfort. Not realizing what had happened, and being focused on her guests, John's mother stopped him before he could reach her. With a stern look and very serious tone she said, *"I'm not interested."* It stopped John in his tracks. He felt terribly rejected. With his heart heavy and his head hung low, he wandered to his room and cried himself to sleep.

Today John talks with many customers who don't have need for his product. The rejection he faces is usually not a problem. But from time to time when the prospect says no he feels terribly hurt. He realizes that this hurt is unwarranted, but he feels it anyway and can't figure out why. Unknown to him, when a prospect uses the exact words, "I'm not interested," it triggers a similar emotional response to the one he had years ago.

Being aware that conditioned emotional responses exist helps explain why you may sometimes feel a strong negative emotion that has no obvious cause. It's not important that you be able to trace the emotion back to something that happened in your childhood. It's enough just to know that the emotion may not be directly tied to the event that triggered it. An important facet of emotional causes begins to emerge here: *emotions have more to do with what's happening inside you than with the triggering event.*

Cause #2: *Emotions Created by Meaning*

Emotions are triggered by external events. But events have no meaning in and of themselves. Through the process of perception, you *create* meanings for events in your environment.

Suppose you were staying late at the office and your spouse called. He or she asks, "When are you coming home?" Different interpretations will cause different emotional reactions. One person might feel that they were being checked up on, that their spouse didn't trust them. They would interpret the call as limiting their freedom, and become angry. Someone else might interpret the question as a symbol that their spouse really cared for them and looked forward to their coming home. This meaning increases their value or importance and would cause them to feel emotions like *warmth* or *love*.

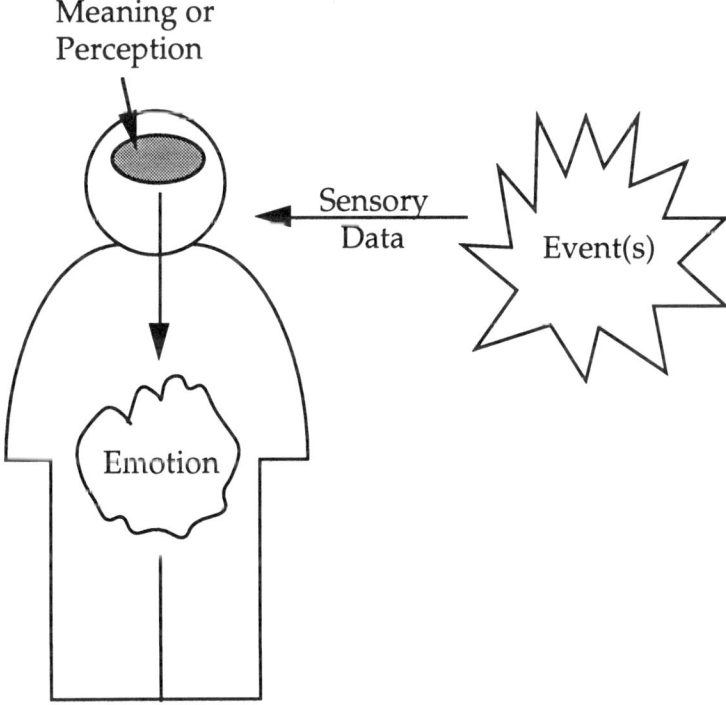

Figure 7.2: The Process of Perception

As you can see in figure 7.2, we become aware of an event through our senses. Next we create a perception (based on past experiences, assumptions, prejudices, etc.) about what the event *means* to us. And it is this meaning that triggers our emotional reaction. This process happens very quickly, below the threshold of consciousness. However, unlike conditioned responses we are not just remembering an old emotional response, we are interpreting a current event and deciding on a current meaning.

In its purest form "meaning" is simply an assessment of whether an event gives us more or less of some fundamental need. At a basic level we all have similar needs. Some of our basic needs include:

- food, water, shelter
- security
- freedom
- physical safety
- status/importance

Negative emotions are triggered when we perceive an event to give us *less* of one of our basic needs. Note that I said when we *perceive* an event to give us less of one of these needs. It's interesting that what one person interprets as reducing a basic need, another may interpret as increasing the same need.

The dangerous thing about the process of perception is that, real as it may seem, the meaning we create may have no basis in reality. As we saw in the example of the phone call from a spouse, there are at least two seemingly logical, rational meanings that can be drawn from an event. The truth is, there are a limitless number of possible interpretations to any event.

Here again we see that it is our processing of the event, more than the event itself, that causes negative emotions. Though it's difficult to intervene in the process of conditioned responses, emotions created by current perceptions are very manageable. We'll look at ways to manage meaning later in this chapter.

Cause #3: *Physical State*

Few people would argue that physical state has a large effect on behavior and emotions. Low blood sugar causes us to feel sluggish, a lack of sleep makes us irritable, and having a cold drains our energy. Physical state is not usually a direct cause, but rather an important influencing factor to many of the emotions we experience.

Have you ever come home from work tired and snapped at your spouse over something that normally wouldn't have bothered you? Ever become irritated with your children when you weren't feeling well? Felt abnormally hurt by a prospect's rejection because you were exhausted by previous stresses of the day? These are all examples of physical ailments contributing to or causing negative emotions. An impaired physical state leads to an impaired emotional response.

For the third time we see an emotional cause that is independent of the triggering event. Though the exact cause of emotions are often very hard to define, there is one important distinction we can make.

Important Distinction:

> *Emotions have more to do with what's happening inside you than the external event that triggered them.*

Actually, this is very good news. We will never be able to control all the events in our environment, but we can control to a large extent what happens inside us. But it is oh so hard to remember that distinction when you are in the midst of a deep emotional reaction. When you're angry, hurt, or depressed, everything is seen through that emotion. It's hard to maintain perspective. Your emotional response may be based on past experience, your subjective perception of the situation, and/or your current physical state. The pivotal key for mastering emotions is the ability to realize, *while you are experiencing the emotion*, that what you are feeling may very well have nothing to do with the event that triggered it. The only way to maintain this kind of perspective in the midst of a deep emotional response is to cultivate a heightened awareness of those negative emotions that we experience most often and that cause us the most harm.

Identifying Your Debilitating Emotions:

Human beings are amazing creatures. Over two billion on the planet and not any two exactly alike. We're different in the way we look, the things we eat, the places we live, *and* the emotions we experience. Though we all share the same basic emotions, the depth and frequency of these emotions is unique to every individual. The first step in managing negative emotions is to clearly define those that affect you the most. Eighty-percent of the battle is awareness.

Think back over the past 10 days. During the time you spent on the job, think about the times you felt least in control and accomplished the least. What emotions caused or contributed to this? Listed below are eight emotions that regularly affect activity-based salespeople. Use the list to help you identify some of your regularly occurring negative emotions. Also consider other emotions that may not be on this list.

Overwhelm - feeling like you have more to do than you could possibly accomplish in the available time.

Frustration - having a clear goal that seems to be within reach, yet not being able to reach it.

Lethargy - lacking motivation, being indifferent to your goals, not caring what happens.

Depression - feeling down, unhappy with your circumstances, and not having the motivation or desire to change those circumstances.

Anxiety/Worry - a painful uneasiness over a defined or undefined problem (i.e. not making this months numbers).

Rejection/Hurt - a feeling of being unwanted or unaccepted; questioning your self-worth.

Disappointment - expecting that something good will happen and then finding out that it did not (i.e. loosing a big sale).

Guilt - feeling that you have done something wrong; feeling that you have not done something that you should have done.

When you read that list you probably think to yourself, "I'm in big trouble. I've got 'em *all*." Don't feel too bad. Everyone, salesperson or not, experiences all these emotions from time to time. But if you're like most people, two or three of these will jump out at you as things that affect you much more often than the others.

The purpose of this exercise is to raise your awareness of these emotions. In order to apply the techniques that follow, you have to recognize limiting emotions when they occur. You need to "catch yourself in the act." And the best way to do that is to clearly define your most frequently occurring negative emotions before they strike. When you are experiencing one of these emotions, you want to be able to step back and with some emotional detachment say, "Oh, this isn't the end of the world, I'm just experiencing (blank)."

The clearer you are about your limiting emotions and what causes them, the more likely you will be to catch yourself in the act. I think it is very helpful to take the time to write a paragraph or two about each of your most harmful emotions. In your writing, include the following.

1. A description of the emotion.
2. What typically triggers the emotion.
3. The negative effects this emotion has for you.

When I look back on my recent past, I know that *the* emotion that has had the greatest negative impact on my performance is what I call "overwhelm." Overwhelm is generated by viewing the work I have as a huge ominous task that can never be completed. This leads me to a "hiding" behavior. I hide from the task by loosing myself in smaller, less important tasks. I wrote the following about overwhelm:

Description - Overwhelm is the feeling of having so much to do that I could never possibly do it all. It makes me feel a pressure in my chest and stomach, and it generates such great fear and stress that I end up doing nothing at all.

Triggers - My overwhelm is triggered by having a lot of projects with many unknowns in them. If I don't know how much work is involved, I imagine the worst. When I begin to mentally stack these projects one on top of the other, along with all the little tasks I have, I create a mental mountain of work.

Negative Effects - Overwhelm is a destroyer of motivation. Seeing things as huge projects takes all the fun out of doing them. Instead of rolling up my sleeves and diving in, I hide in smaller, safer activity. I work less overall hours and am more tired at the end of the day. The mental stress I generate drains my physical energy. I wait until the last minute to get started, and then, under great pressure, complete things on time. This is a very painful process, and I usually find the task wasn't as hard or as large as I had imagined it to be.

I can't overstate the value of doing this exercise. Writing about your emotions will give you clarity about the exact nature of these emotions and raise your awareness so that you can catch yourself in the midst of a deep emotional response. I recommend that you take some time now, or after you finish the chapter, to go through this process for your most limiting emotions.

Techniques for Managing Emotions

When I first wrote this section it was titled "Techniques for *Controlling* Emotions." I changed the title because I don't believe we can ever completely control our emotions. I'm not sure we would want to. Emotions are part of what make us alive. I don't believe we can turn negative emotions off like a light switch, but by applying some simple management techniques, we can reduce their frequency and severity. The following are the most universally applicable and consistently effective techniques I've found.

Before You Try Any "Technique" ...

... identify the cause. Ask yourself, "What is it about <u>blank</u> (the triggering event) that makes me feel so <u>blank</u> (emotional response)?" Look deeply for the answer to that question. It's amazing how much better you feel when you get a clear definition of what caused the emotion. Application of the techniques that follow can be extremely powerful if you understand the root of your emotion. But if you don't, they can seem hollow, like putting a band-aid on a severed artery. If you're not clear on the cause you'll have a feeling of, "How long will this solution last?" and "Will the emotion resurface?"

A few weeks ago I was at the Christmas party for my wife's company. We'd had a long day, we had been at the party for almost four hours, it was late, and I was ready to go. I said something to my wife about leaving and she responded by changing the subject. I immediately felt a flash of extreme anger. I didn't show what I was feeling, but got up and went to the men's room, just to get away from the situation. As I was stepping through the door, I was curious. What was it about what she said that made me *so* angry? The answer came screaming into my head, *"Nothing!"* There was nothing wrong with her response. Certainly nothing warranting the anger I felt. Then suddenly it hit me, "You're tired. Very tired." It had been a long day before the party, I'd just spent several hours meeting and mingling with people I didn't know, and it was nearly midnight. I was physically and mentally fatigued. Almost instantly came an overwhelming sense of relief. There was nothing wrong with her, and nothing wrong with me. It was a simple case of being tired. A good night's sleep would cure everything. I walked back to the table with a spring in my step and a song in heart. It was no big deal. I was just tired.

Actually, identifying the cause of your negative emotions is itself a technique. But I wanted to give it special emphasis because it is always, always, *always* the technique you should apply first. After you have identified the cause, the techniques that follow will be more than enough to put you back in the emotional driver's seat.

Technique #1: *Manage the Meaning*

In the 1984 presidential campaign, incumbent Ronald Reagan was running against Walter Mondale. One of the issues Mondale began to raise in the campaign was Reagan's age. It was a real issue. Reagan was in his 70's, his head shook as he talked, he was frail, and he looked *old*. During one of the debates, Mondale made a particularly poignant comment about Reagan's advancing years. The moderator turned to Reagan and said, "Mr. President, would you care to respond to Mr. Mondale's comment?" Reagan paused for a moment, looked at the audience, back at the moderator, then back to the audience and said, "Mr. Moderator, I refuse to make a campaign issue of my opponent's *youth and inexperience*." The audience erupted in laughter and completely forgot Mondale's comment.

Reagan had cleverly changed the meaning, and with it the emotions it created. In essence, Mondale was saying , "See this piece of information, it *means* Reagan is too old." Reagan said, "No. See this same piece of information, it means Mondale is too young."

As we said earlier, one of the primary causes of emotions is the meaning we assign to events. If you want to change an emotion, you need only change the meaning. As we saw in the example above, changing the meaning can totally transform a situation in an instant.

When an event occurs that triggers a negative emotion, it is often caused by the way you are viewing the event. In order to change the meaning, you want to find a different way to look at the same situation. The good news is, when you find a new viewpoint it can change your emotions *immediately*. You can assist yourself in the process of looking for a better meaning by answering the following questions:

Table 7.1: Questions That Shift Meaning

1. What's good about this situation?
2. What's humorous about this event?
3. Is it really that bad? What's the worst thing that could happen?
4. How important will this event be in five years? Ten years?
5. It could have been worse, at least I didn't _____.
6. What's the opportunity here?

Write these questions on a card and carry it with you. Next time you catch yourself in a negative emotion, pull out the card and take a few minutes to answer the questions. If you seriously try to find an answer, you'll be amazed at how well this works.

Technique #2: *Change Your Body*

The mind and body are intimately connected. The things we are feeling and thinking internally are always exhibited externally through posture, breathing, facial expressions, and movement. A person who is depressed doesn't move as fast, breath as deep, or hold their head as high as someone who just won the lottery.

In a study done in 1974, college students were instructed to frown. "Pull your eyebrows together," "Turn the corners of your mouth down." With no other triggering event, these students reported feeling angry. On the other hand, those who were instructed to smile reported feeling happier and found cartoons and jokes more amusing than students who were not consciously controlling their facial expressions.

In another study, students were instructed to put pained expressions on their faces while watching test subjects receive electric shocks. Compared to students who were not manipulating on their faces, the test group experienced greater heart rates and increased perspiration.[3] Laboratory evidence confirms that consciously controlling the body does have a direct impact on emotions.

I remember seeing a cartoon when I was young about a boy named Sherman and a dog named Mr. Peabody. Mr. Peabody was a unique dog. He wore big glasses, spoke perfect English, and had an I.Q. of 150. As Sherman and Peabody would have adventures each week, Mr. Peabody was always coming up with clever and creative solutions to save the day. In one episode they were in an auto race against the villain. If they lost, the heroine would die, or the villain would escape with the money, or something like that. Beginning the last lap, Sherman and Peabody were behind in the race. Sherman said frantically, "Mr. Peabody, Mr. Peabody, we're losing! What are we going to do?"

"Oh it's quite simple Sherman," Peabody says in his unflappable, matter-of-fact tone. He reaches down and breaks the glass on the speedometer, and with his paw moves the needle from 80 to 120 miles per hour. As Peabody said later while describing the race to the heroine, "... and as I moved the needle, *naturally* the car went faster and we won the race."

Okay, maybe this would only work in a cartoon, but it illustrates the principle. The things we often think of as cause and effect sometimes work in reverse, effect leads to cause. Our minds control our bodies and our bodies control our minds.

When you're feeling depressed or lethargic or hurt, try changing your body to change the emotion. Next time you want to change an emotion quickly, try the following:

Move - Stand-up, take a walk, jump around. Move your body

---

[3] *Psychology*, pages 296-297.

differently than the way you are currently moving it. Unpleasant emotions with low arousal tend to be accompanied by very slow movements. Get up and move differently if you want to feel differently.

Stand-Up Straight - Shoulders back, eyes forward, head up. A great deal of how we feel is held in our posture. You'll often find yourself slumping when you're feeling sad, hurt, or depressed. Consciously change your posture and watch the effects it has on your emotions. Stand the way you would if you were a war hero about to receive the medal of honor.

Smile - As noted earlier in the studies on smiling, facial expressions not only communicate a great deal about our emotions but also have a causative effect. If you want to change your mood, change your face. Tilt your head back, open your eyes wide, and smile. Act like you just won the lottery. If this feels silly, that's good. It means you're doing it right.

Breathe - People who are sad or depressed tend to breathe shallowly. They take small breaths from the chest instead of deep breaths from the diaphragm. Take a few deep breaths next time you're feeling a little down and see if you don't immediately feel better.

Technique #3: *Manage Your Environment*

Your immediate environment may be affecting your emotions more than you realize. Next time you're experiencing a negative emotion ...

Take a Break - Get out of the environment and situation that triggered the emotion. Take a walk. Try not to think about the event during the break. Think about your family, or a favorite vacation spot, or some hobby you enjoy.

Listen to Music - Music has magical qualities for creating positive emotions. Upbeat, energizing music tends to make us feel more positive and energized. Serene, calm music tends to relax us. There have been many times when I've blasted the stereo with Huey Lewis or Linda Ronstadt to get myself going. I feel energized almost instantly. Experiment with some of your favorite energizing and/or relaxing music. Listen to it often. It may become one of your favorite tools for managing negative emotions.

Technique #4: *Get Some Perspective*

Negative emotions feed on themselves because they trigger irrational thoughts which perpetuate the emotion. We often continue to stew and simmer over something that really isn't that important. When you find yourself struggling to break out of an emotion, it's time to get some perspective, change your focus, and come back to the situation with a clearer head. When you need to change your perspective, try the following:

Talk to Someone - One of the best ways to get an outside perspective is to simply tell someone you trust what has happened and how you're feeling about it. The listener's job is not to tell you what you should feel or do. They are simply there to listen, ask a few questions, and offer another perspective. I often use my wife as a sounding board by asking her, "Am I seeing this right?" or "How could I think about this differently so it wouldn't seem so difficult?" It's easy to get so close to problems that you can't see the situation rationally. Other people are a great resource for finding new perspectives.

Write in a Journal - Without a doubt, the greatest source of clear thinking is writing. Getting things down on paper puts problems in front of you where you can see them. It's hard to hold on to grossly irrational thoughts when you see them on paper.

Don't be too worried about the structure of writing in a journal every day or having a special book to write in, just get a yellow pad and go at it. Experiment and have fun with it. And don't just write about the situation, but also about your *feelings*. It's amazing how therapeutic putting your feelings on paper can be. I've been keeping a journal for over 14 years, and consider it one of my most valued emotional management tools.

Just let it go - Sometimes the fastest and easiest way to respond to a triggering event is to just let it pass. In essence saying to yourself, "Yes, I know this would normally cause me to feel very (hurt, angry, or depressed), but this time I'm just going to let it pass. Next time it happens I'll allow myself to feel extra hurt. But I don't have time for this right now. I'll just let it go." Imagine putting the triggering event and your emotions in the basket of a hot air balloon. Watch it drift softly and silently into the afternoon sky. Let it pass. Just let this one go.

These are obviously not *all* the techniques available to manage emotions. The techniques I selected for this chapter are those with the broadest applicability and those that are the most reliable. Use the ones you like, change them, combine them, and explore some of your own. But please remember the most important technique of all, getting clear on why this event caused this emotion.

The key now is going to be your willingness to use these techniques when you aren't thinking too rationally.

Implementing the Techniques

Before you can implement any of the above techniques you have to recognize when you are experiencing a negative emotion. In a heated moment of anger or in the depths of depression, when it feels like the world is coming to an end, you have to be able to say to yourself, "Hey, wait a minute. This is just an emotion." Only then can you take conscious action to change it.

But having that kind of rational thinking in the midst of an emotion is easier said than done. You have to have your antenna up and have a heightened awareness of those emotions that effect you most. The best way to do this is to go through the exercise described earlier to identify your most common limiting emotions. By identifying them in advance you will have a fighting chance to recognize a negative emotion when it strikes.

Once you realize you are experiencing a negative emotion, you will have a split second of sanity in which you have the opportunity to take control and apply some of the techniques we've covered. But will you want to? Remember, you're angry, *really* angry. What's to keep you from saying, "To hell with it. I'm damn mad, and I'm going to stay damn mad!"?

The truth is, there's really nothing to keep you from saying this. That's why this split second of sanity is such a precarious position, so fleeting. Use your moment of sanity to try to channel the arousal you're feeling into curiosity. Ask yourself, "What exactly is it about (blank) that makes me feel so (blank)?" Be as determined to find an answer to that question as you were to feel angry about the situation.

When you've identified what you believe to be the cause, ask yourself these three questions.

Table 7.2: Implementation Questions

1. Do I want to feel this way?
2. Who controls my emotions?
3. What technique, strategy, or method can I use right now to help me make it through the next few minutes?

Question #1 presupposes that you have a choice. By answering, you're admitting that it's within your power to *choose* to feel another way. In those cases where your answer is, "No, I don't want to feel this way," you've taken the first step toward changing how you're feeling by acknowledging that you would like to feel something different.

Negative emotions have a purpose and sometimes it's healthy to experience them. You shouldn't feel like you always have to use the techniques described in this chapter. If a close family member died, you would certainly need a time of mourning to get through the experience healthfully. There may well be times when you'll answer, "Yes, I do want to feel this way." And in those cases, give yourself some more time. But many, many times the emotions we're experiencing aren't a needed venting of internal conflict. We aren't purging internal stress, we're generating it with irrational thoughts.

Question #2 reminds you that *you* are in control. The answer you want to give is, "I do! I control what I'm feeling and I can choose to change it." If you control your emotions then you can choose to make them something different. Someone else doesn't dictate your response. Events don't. You do.

Question #3 is obviously designed to access techniques that will help you get past this limiting emotion. Think back on the techniques we've covered in this chapter and apply one in this situation. Don't be concerned about trying to completely squelch the emotion. Sometimes it is too much to ask to eliminate it entirely. Simply look for a technique that will help you side-step this feeling for the moment.

Q&A:

Q: How quickly will I see a noticeable difference in my ability to manage my emotions?

A: Managing emotions is a skill. And like any skill, you only get better with practice. The more you practice, the sooner you'll master these techniques. The key here is cultivating the ability to *recognize a limiting emotion when you are in the midst of it*. When you're angry, frustrated, or depressed you don't always think clearly. By taking some time to identify and describe the negative emotions that effect you most, you'll be much more likely to recognize them when they strike. If you practice these techniques every time you experience a negative emotion, you should develop a high skill level in 3-4 weeks.

Q: What if I don't feel like using these techniques?

A: You probably won't. If you are really angry, and someone reminds you to use some technique, it would probably just make you more angry. The key is to realize that the emotion you are experiencing is not necessarily appropriate, it is just *one possible option* for the situation. Remember the first question from the section on implementing these techniques, "Do I want to feel this way?" This question is designed to remind you that you have a choice. In those times when your answer is, "Your damn right I want to feel this way," allow yourself some more time. But, in those times when your answer is, "Well, I guess I don't really *want* to feel this way," you can begin to apply some of the techniques we've discussed here.

Q: Is there ever a time when it is appropriate to feel depressed, frustrated, or angry?

A: Yes. Absolutely yes. Negative emotions are part of life. It's only natural that we feel depressed or angry sometimes. What we want to do is counteract irrational thoughts which unnecessarily prolong a negative response. I don't want you to feel guilty for being depressed or frustrated. Just know that you have options and when appropriate you can apply some of these techniques to help you come out of it.

Q: Can I really turn a strong negative emotion into a strong positive one?

A: Yes. Sometimes I believe you can. Changing the meaning can sometimes completely turn an event around, and therefore your response. But this is not the aim of this chapter. I hope the ideas and techniques I've suggested will help you moderate negative emotions. I hope they will help you feel somewhat positive, or at least neutral about what would have previously thrown you into a fit of frustration or depression. If that is our only result from this chapter, to moderate your emotions, we have been greatly successful.

Application Exercises

1. Take five minutes and identify the negative emotions that affect you the most. What triggers them? What are their negative effects?

2. Discuss the limiting emotions you identified with a friend or colleague. This discussion will give you additional clarity and heighten your awareness when these emotions hit you. You'll be surprised at how much other people experience the same emotions.

3. Write the "Questions that Shift Meaning" from table 7.1 on a card and carry it with you. Next time you are experiencing one of your limiting emotions, pull out the card and talk yourself through the questions.

Chapter 8

Tracking

"My mother drew a distinction between achievement and success. She said that achievement is the knowledge that you have studied and worked hard and done the best that is in you. Success is being praised by others, and that's nice too, but not as important or satisfying."

-- Helen Hayes

One of the key measures of my sales effort has always been the number of phone calls I make each week. If I simply pick up the phone a certain number of times every week, my long-term sales goals are easily realized. But many, MANY times, goals that were very reachable, goals that were within my grasp, ended up slipping *through* my grasp because I failed to consistently execute my plan. It was too easy to lose sight of the connection between the activity at hand and my long-term goal. I knew my success was dependent on my ability to stay sufficiently motivated over a long period of time, but I just couldn't seem to do it. The goal seemed too far away, too fuzzy, and my motivation waned. I continued to struggle until I discovered one of the least used and most powerful tools for consistent motivation, a little known but very powerful technique called "tracking."

Tracking: the process of recording and monitoring progress toward a goal or objective

You probably do some tracking now. You may call it "record keeping" or "the monthly report" or something else, but in essence it is tracking. Most salespeople track their activity grudgingly (because their manager requires it) or not at all, citing it as boring, time consuming, or downright anal retentive. If you feel that way, I'm going to ask you to set aside that view for just a moment. In this chapter I want to share with you some reasons why I believe tracking is an incredibly powerful motivator as well as some techniques that will help you maximize its benefits.

Shaping Behavior Through Positive Reinforcement

When I was growing up in my hometown near Houston, Texas, every couple of years my family would take a day trip to Searama Marine World in Galveston. Searama is a marine park like the Aquarium in Boston or San Francisco. I always enjoyed looking through the thick glass windows at the sharks and rays and giant groupers in the big viewing tank. I remember that Searama had a giant sea turtle exhibit and even an alligator wrestling show. But the thing I loved most was, without a doubt, the trained dolphin show.

The audience sat in bleachers alongside an outdoor tank where the dolphin would talk with the trainer in its high squeaky voice, dance on it's tail, and, as the grand finale, jump through a hoop 15 feet above the surface the water. I was fascinated by the way the dolphin swam several laps around the tank building up speed, then came bursting through the surface and rose 15 feet into the air and straight through the hoop. If I were in a tank of water 20 feet deep, I could barely keep my head up, much less spring 15 feet above the surface. It wasn't until I learned how the dolphin is trained to make that jump that I realized what a great lesson in motivation it is.

After the dolphin is brought in from the ocean, it is put in the big tank and allowed to swim around for a while. When it becomes comfortable in its new environment, the trainer places a large hoop in the tank about half way up from the bottom. By the law of averages the dolphin will sometimes swim through the hoop, and sometimes beside the hoop. The trainer stands by watching, holding a bucket of small fish. Every time the dolphin swims through the hoop, the trainer throws a fish in the tank as a small reward. If the dolphin swims beside the hoop, it doesn't get a fish. Through the hoop a fish, beside the hoop no fish. Through, fish. Beside, no fish. Being a smart animal, it isn't long until the dolphin is swimming through the hoop every time. At this point the trainer gradually raises the hoop until it's at the surface of the water and the dolphin is making small jumps to get through it. Eventually the hoop is raised 15 feet above the surface and, on cue, the dolphin makes several loops around the perimeter of the tank, then bursts out of the water and straight through the hoop.

The method the trainer uses to get the dolphin to gradually swim through the hoop more and more often is called behavior "shaping." Shaping the dolphin's behavior by rewarding desired behavior is called "positive reinforcement." The principle of positive reinforcement states that behaviors that are reinforced (i.e. generate positive consequences) tend to be perpetuated, and behaviors that are not reinforced tend to go away or become "extinguished." Psychologist B. F. Skinner conducted a great deal of research on the applications of reinforcement. Skinner and his followers assert that all human behavior can be explained through the principle of positive and negative reinforcement.

If you think of anything you do on a regular basis (brush your teeth, go to work, even make your bed), with some thought you will find a positive reinforcer at work perpetuating the behavior. Brushing your teeth maintains your health, going to work gives you money, and if you're as retentive as I am, making your bed gives you a sense of accomplishment. If you are rewarded for undesirable behaviors, these behaviors will be perpetuated also. If you spend too much time around the coffee pot talking to your buddies, it's because you are in some way rewarded for that behavior. It feels good to talk with your friends, especially when the alternative is picking up the telephone. If a behavior continues it is somewhere being reinforced.

How can positive reinforcement be used to increase sales activity? Unlike other animals, human beings are mental creatures. The most powerful rewards, either positive or negative, occur between our ears. What we need is a *bucket of mental fish* we can use to reward desirable behaviors. Tracking is that bucket of mental fish.

Tracking as a Means of Positive Reinforcement

One of the most difficult things an activity-based salesperson has to do is to execute the same repetitive sales activities day in and day out. And the way most of us have been taught to deal with this difficulty is to remind ourselves that our daily activities are necessary to reach our long-term goals. We've been taught to think, "I have to make these calls if I want that BMW" or, "I have to do this paperwork if I want to make the mortgage." What we are doing by thinking these thoughts is trying to motivate ourselves to execute our daily activities. This line of thinking is what's known as "delayed gratification." We put off rewards today for the promise of greater rewards tomorrow. And although this is a very popular motivational strategy, I believe its ability to motivate day in and day out is limited. Using the delayed gratification strategy, we are always trying to get ourselves to do something we don't want to do *today* so that *someday* we might have what we want. The problem is, if you have to work a long time for the prospect of some distant reward it's easy to decide that the reward isn't worth the effort.

A better strategy would be to motivate ourselves not with a distant reward, but with immediate rewards for daily activity. We need reinforcement for the most basic sales behaviors (finding new prospects, picking up the phone, preparing proposals, etc.) if we are going to be successful as activity-based salespeople. We need to have someone standing in our office with a dripping bucket, throwing us a fish every time we pick up the phone. Okay, unless you really love sardines, this type of reward probably won't work. But the principle of positive reinforcement says that we continue to execute behaviors that are immediately rewarded. Somehow we've got to get immediate rewards for daily activity. I think I've discovered a way to do this that won't leave your office smelling like a fishery. It's all about keeping a continuous score.

If you've ever played golf, you're probably familiar with the old adage, "It's the one good shot that keeps you coming back." It means that you could play terribly, but if you hit one long straight drive, or sink one 30 foot putt, the satisfaction from that event is more than enough to make you want to endure the frustration all over again. If you're shooting baskets and you swish one from the top of the key, the feeling you get when it goes "swish" makes you want to try again. The feeling of satisfaction generated by these positive outcomes could be thought of as "mental fish." *And these mental fish have far more power to motivate human beings than actual fish will ever have to motivate a dolphin.* Suppose you set a goal to make 20 calls each day, and defined your positive outcome as simply completing all 20 calls (*not as making a sale*). If you keep a continuous log of the number of calls you make, then with each call you get a small feeling of satisfaction or a mental fish. Even if your results aren't what you'd hoped for, you will be getting rewarded for one of the most important behaviors any activity-based salesperson can possess: *picking up the phone*. The process of keeping score, what I call "tracking," provides positive reinforcement even if you aren't closing any sales.

Suppose you've just arrived and taken your seat in the stands for game seven of the NBA Finals. As you sit down, you notice that something looks strange about the court below. You stare at it for a few minutes and then realize what's different, there is no scoreboard. You ask the people seated around you why the scoreboard has been removed, but they're as confused as you are. About 10 minutes before tip-off, the NBA Commissioner walks to center court with a microphone. He explains that the owners have decided to make a few changes in the game. No longer will there be a record kept of the number of baskets that are made. Instead, the winner will be determined by a group of judges who will observe the teams, and after an hour or so of play, choose a winner based on style, artistic interpretation, good sportsmanship, and the like.

What's wrong with this picture? Okay, it's stupid. Really STUPID! Why would anyone do such a thing? This is suppose to be a *game*. Who would want to play a game if you didn't keep score? The score is what creates moment-to-moment motivation and makes the game fun. Without keeping score the game would be horribly boring. If the game is basketball, you've got to keep track of the baskets made. If the game is hockey, you've got to know how many pucks go into the net. And if the game is sales, you've got to have some method of keeping a moment-to-moment score. Don't you? Otherwise it would be horribly boring. Wouldn't it? If your daily sales activities: making calls, writing letters, and preparing proposals, have ever seemed tedious or boring to you, maybe it's because you're not keeping a continuous score.

How to Use Tracking as a Motivational Tool

Tracking is simply the process of keeping a continuous log of the activity you want to manage. In this section we will discuss two tools for tracking sales behavior: activity logs and time logs. Though there are an infinite number of activities you could track, if you just want to know the number of times you've done something (i.e. calls you've made, letters you've mailed, or proposals you've prepared), the process will be the same regardless of the activity. In the example that follows I will use phone calls as the activity to be managed, but a similar process can be used for any activity.

Activity Logs (Example: The Phone Log)

Figure 8.1 shows a phone log in its simplest form. Here the salesperson is just keeping track of the number of dials she makes each day. Because this log is set up for a one week time frame, we can assume she is tracking progress toward her weekly goal for outbound phone calls. Most of your tracking should be connected to the weekly targets you set for key sales activities in chapter 4.

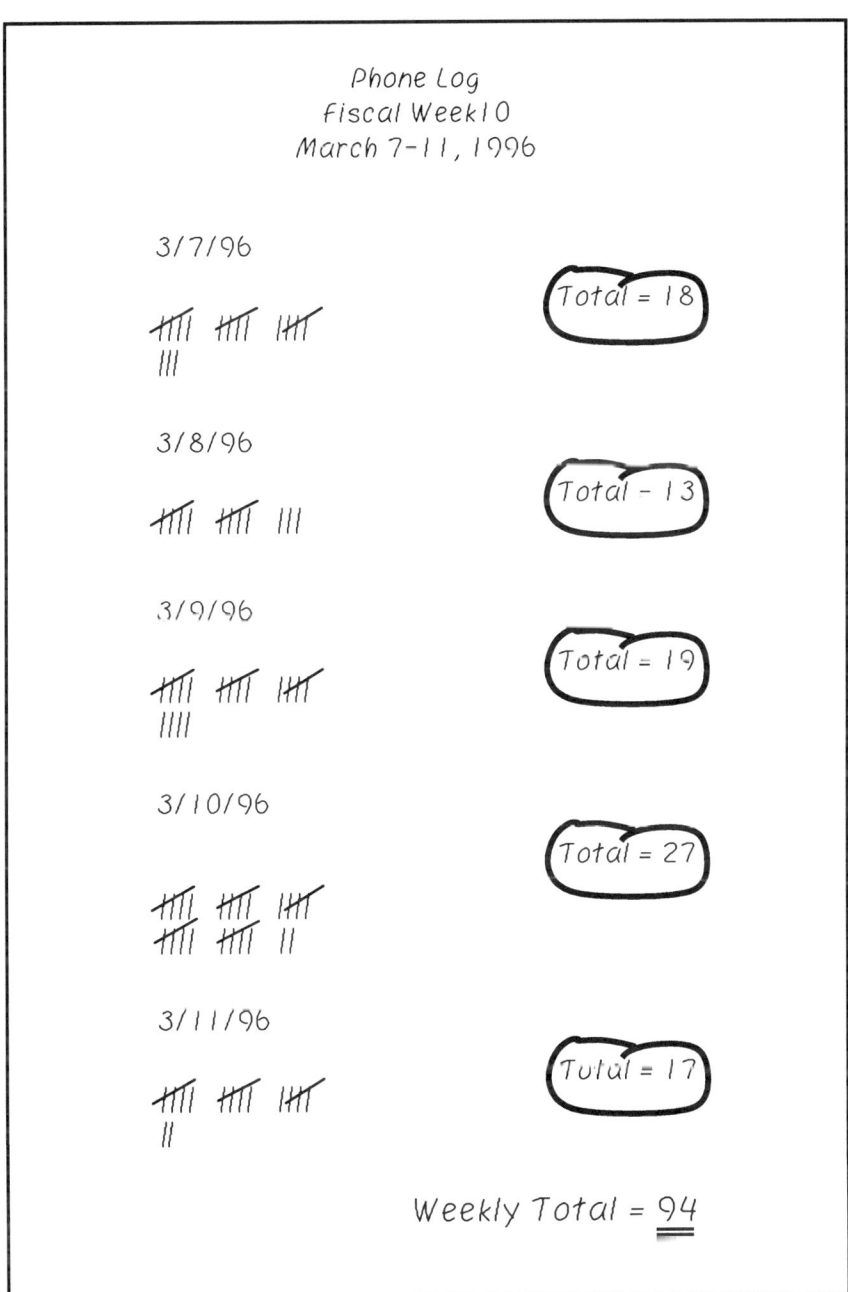

Figure 8.1: Simple Phone Log

I caution those who want to do their tracking solely through the contact management system on their computer. Remember, what we want here is a *continuous, visual log*. Most contact management systems only tell you how many calls you've made when you ask, usually at the end of the day. That's about as much fun as knowing the score of the basketball game long after it's over. I'm a big advocate of the manual log, a piece of paper on which you make a small mark each time you complete a tiny step toward your goal. There is significant motivational value to physically taking a pen or pencil and making a tick mark. Some will say it takes too much time to keep a manual log. I disagree. It doesn't take any extra time, but even if it did it wouldn't matter. This isn't about efficiency, *it's about motivation*. I'd rather be 95% efficient and motivated to make 4 hours of phone calls than 100% efficient but lose motivation after 10 minutes.

Beyond simply being a motivational tool, one of the additional benefits tracking provides is the ability to use the data you collect to refine your sales technique and increase your effectiveness. In figure 8.2 we see a slightly more detailed phone log that segments data into prospect classes and results codes. Here the salesperson is tracking his calls to three classes of prospects which are listed across the top of the log. "New" stands for calls made to prospects who have never been contacted before, "Follow" for follow-up calls to previously contacted prospects, and "Other" for any calls that don't fit into the first two categories (i.e. servicing existing clients). Later, when the salesperson analyzes his data, this information will help him know if he's spending enough time pursuing new business versus contacting existing customers. Another possibility would be to track prospect classes by income range as shown in figure 8.3. If you're frustrated because you aren't bringing in enough big accounts, track income classes and look at where you are directing your effort. If 80% of your activity is directed at low income clients, you can't expect a huge volume of high end sales. Choose the prospect classes you track based on what you want to know about the focus of your activity. I track calls for each of my six target market segments. If I am not doing as well as I would like in one of those

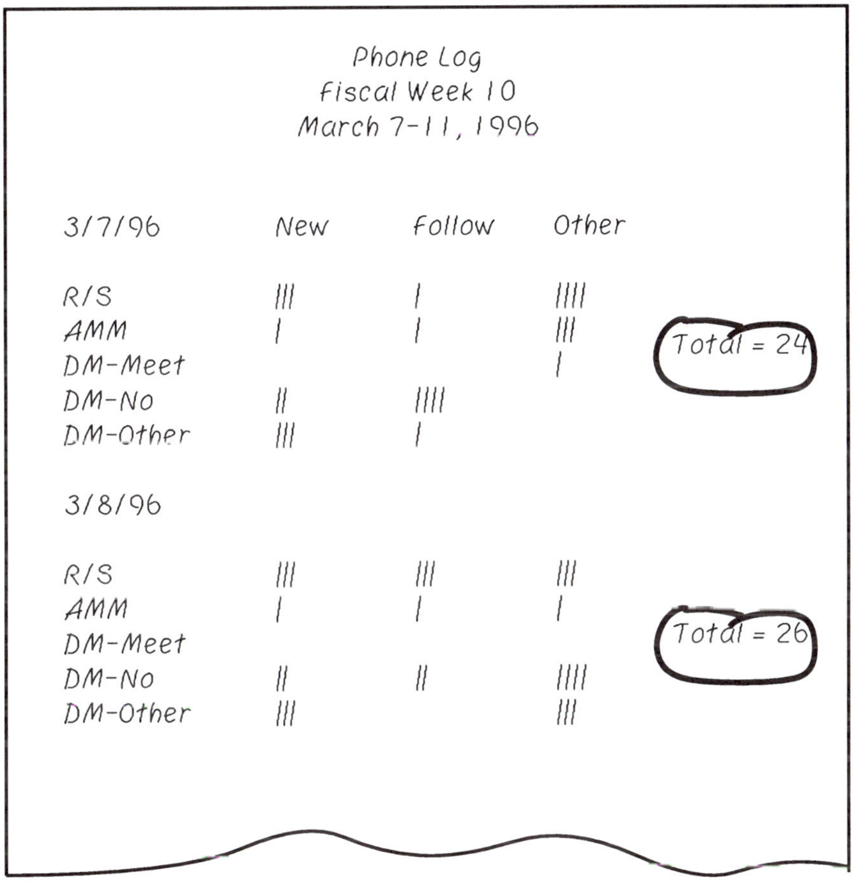

```
                    Phone Log
                  Fiscal Week 10
                  March 7-11, 1996


      3/7/96        New      Follow     Other

      R/S           |||        |        ||||
      AMM           |          |        |||
      DM-Meet                           |          Total = 24
      DM-No         ||        ||||
      DM-Other      |||        |

      3/8/96

      R/S           |||       |||       |||
      AMM           |          |        |
      DM-Meet                                      Total = 26
      DM-No         ||         ||       ||||
      DM-Other      |||                 |||
```

Figure 8.2: Detailed Phone Log

markets, I now have real data about how much effort I've been investing there. The classes you track will be unique to your industry and may require some experimentation before you are capturing the right data.

Look back at figure 8.2 for a moment. Down the left-hand side you will see codes for the results of each call. The codes represent the following:

126 • Activity-Based Selling

R/S   - spoke with receptionist or secretary
AMM   - answering machine, left message
DM-Meet   - spoke to decision maker, agreed to meet with me
DM-No   - spoke to decision maker, declined to meet with me
DM-Other - spoke to decision maker, may meet with me

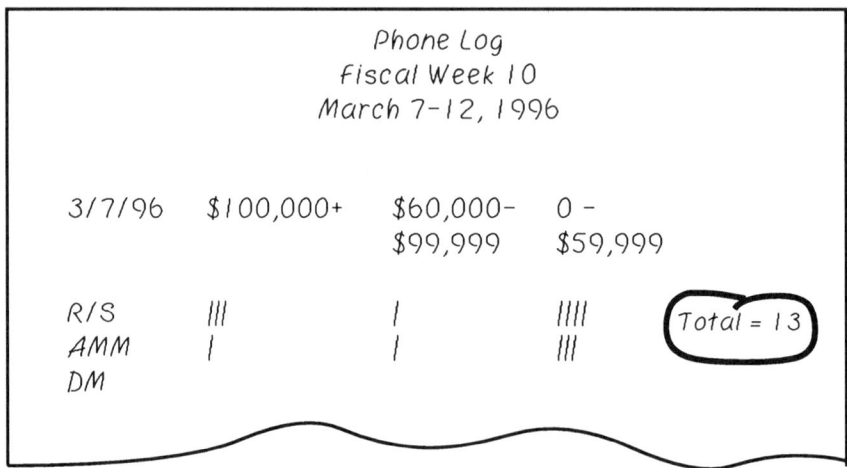

Figure 8.3: Tracking by Income Range

Prospect classes help you analyze the *focus* of your activity. Results codes help you analyze the *effectiveness* of that activity. By looking at the results of your individual calls, you might notice that only one out of ten decision makers you speak with agrees to meet with you. In this case, your telephone persuasion skills may need improving. If you talk to lots of secretaries and few decision makers, you may need to improve your skills at getting through the "gatekeeper," or develop a better strategy for timing the call so you catch decision makers in their office. Again, you will have to experiment to find which codes will give you the most valuable information.

I recommend you *keep these log sheets* in a file or notebook so that at the end of the month and at the end of the year you will know exactly how much activity you've generated. This information will be invaluable when it is time to refine the effectiveness of your activity. We'll talk more about this in chapter 11. I know all this may seem rather complicated, but really it is not. Once you have your log sheets set up, tracking this information will happen automatically.

Remember, the primary goal or tracking is moment-to-moment motivation. If segmenting your data into prospect classes and results codes seems too complicated, then use the simpler version of the phone log shown in figure 8.1. It will have the same motivational effect.

Other Activity Logs

The phone log is representative of any activity log. Similar tracking devices should be used for your other key activities. Depending on your industry, you might consider tracking:

- sales letters mailed
- hours spent developing a prospect list
- number of new prospects added to your list
- proposals sent out within a certain time frame
- applications submitted within a certain time frame
- number of face-to-face sales meetings scheduled

What's important here is to choose those measurements that drive the behaviors you believe will make you successful.

Don't go overboard with tracking. Tracking one or two key activities will be extremely motivating and help you be accountable to your goals. But if you try to track everything, it will become too cumbersome and you'll probably decide it's more effort than it's worth. What you track will direct your focus. You can't track everything, so choose the activities that you believe are most critical to your success. For the beginner, I recommend tracking 2 or 3 key activities, absolutely no more than 5. After you've done it for a while, use your own judgement.

The Time Log

There is one other tracking device that is significantly different from the activity logs we've just discussed. A tool I've found to have great motivational value for me is the *time log*. Unlike other types of tracking, the time log does not count the number of executions of a certain activity. It tracks everything you do every minute of the day. You can see an example of a time log in figure 8.4.

Keeping a time log creates an acute awareness of how you are using every minute of your day. It will make you very aware of exactly how much time you spend at the coffee pot, in personal phone calls, and chatting with colleagues. It's hard to goof off when you're held accountable for every moment.

I had lunch recently with two professors from a local university. I told them about this book and that my goal was to help people create 10-20% more productive activity without putting in any more hours or adding any additional stress to their lives. One of them said, "That sounds great. *Can you do it?*" It was a good question. I had to think for a moment. Then I thought about my own experience as an activity-based salesperson and with a great sense of confidence told him I could *absolutely guarantee* anyone at least a 10% increase in productivity if they will do one thing: keep an accurate written record of everything they do. They both pursed their lips, looked up in thought, then nodded together in agreement and said, "You know what ... you're right."

Most people aren't aware of how much of their time is unproductive. One of the professors told me that the average person is engaged in productive activity only 40-50% of their day. Many people come in at 7:30, work frantically all day, leave the office at 6:00, and complain about how hard they work. The truth is, if you followed them during a typical day you would find that they spent 25 minutes at the coffee pot chatting with their buddies, made 7 personal phone calls consuming a total of 45 minutes, and jumped frantically from one crisis to another without ever finishing anything. When you keep you first time log, you will be shocked at how much of your time is unproductive.

Tracking • 129

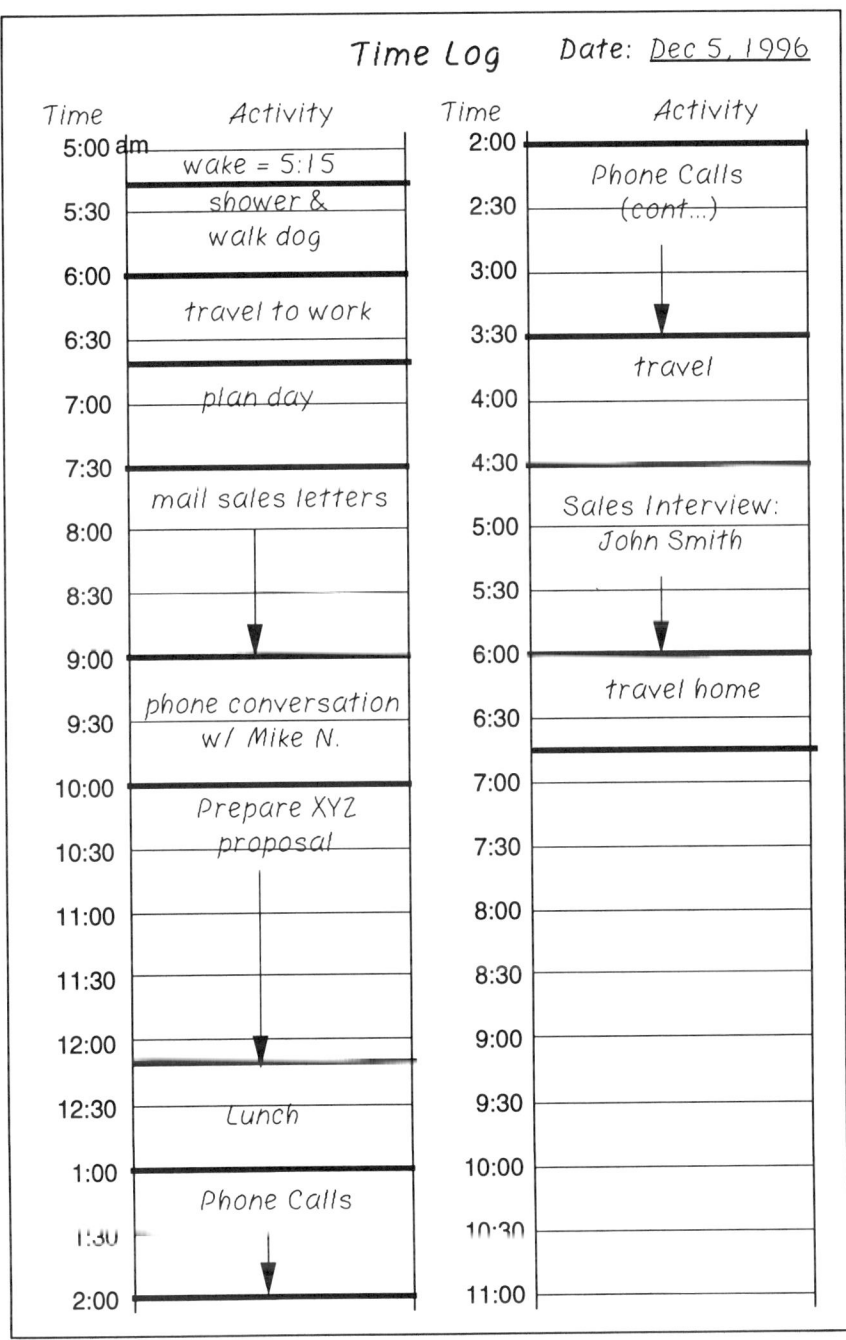

Figure 8.4: The Time Log

Almost every time management seminar or book recommends keeping a time log. Their reasoning is that after you see how you are spending your time, and where you are wasting it, you can make needed corrections. The ability to analyze and refine your activities is always an important *secondary* benefit of tracking. But the primary benefit of any tracking device is its ability to reinforce desired behavior.

When time management experts recommend keeping a time log to analyze and repair your unproductive work habits, they are assuming that the log will give you an accurate picture of your work day. Nothing could be further from the truth. The only way to get an accurate picture of how you are currently using your time is for someone to follow you all day with a video camera *without your knowledge*. If you knew someone was following you with a video camera, would you be as likely to spend a half hour at the coffee pot, make a half hour of personal phone calls, or sit in a colleague's office chatting about last night's ball game? Having someone observe you and make a precise accounting of your actions motivates most people to put on a good show.

A time log is the next best thing to a video camera. It is an accurate accounting of your actions for the day. For most people, this self-awareness and accountability is enough to make *significant* behavioral changes. If you need a little more motivation, you can ask a colleague (spouse, etc.) to spend 10 minutes reviewing you time logs with you at the end of each week. Believe me, if you are honest and record things accurately, there is no way you will spend 30 minutes at the coffee pot knowing someone will see that behavior on your time log.

A message to the time management experts: a time log will never give you an accurate picture of what a person is doing because *the process of recording and being accountable for behavior greatly changes behavior*. The good news for us is that is exactly the goal we seek: changed behavior.

Other Performance Indicators:

Caution! If you're already feeling a little overwhelmed by all this tracking stuff, don't read this section. It's a "bonus section" for those who are willing to keep all this data and who want to squeeze the last ounce of benefit from this motivational tool called tracking.

Tracking is a powerful technique for modifying *any* behavior. You might consider keeping an accurate written record of some other key performance indicators. For me, the following are important indicators of my efforts even though they are not specific sales activities:

- time I get up in the morning
- time I stop working
- time spent in meditation
- time spent writing
- number of times I exercise each week
- what I eat
- time spent reading
- number of people I network with each month
- time spent analyzing and refining my sales presentation
- consistency in setting and monitoring weekly goals.

Though not specific sales activities, doing these things makes me happier and more productive. And for that reason, they are important behaviors to manage.

Don't try to track all these all the time. I track the ones that are most important to me (exercise, writing, weekly goals) all the time. The others I may track for a month or so, stop for a while, then come back to them again later when I feel a need to modify that behavior.

Graphical Display of Data

To really maximize the value of tracking, you can display the data visually, summarizing your progress over several weeks, months, or the entire year.

132 • Activity-Based Selling

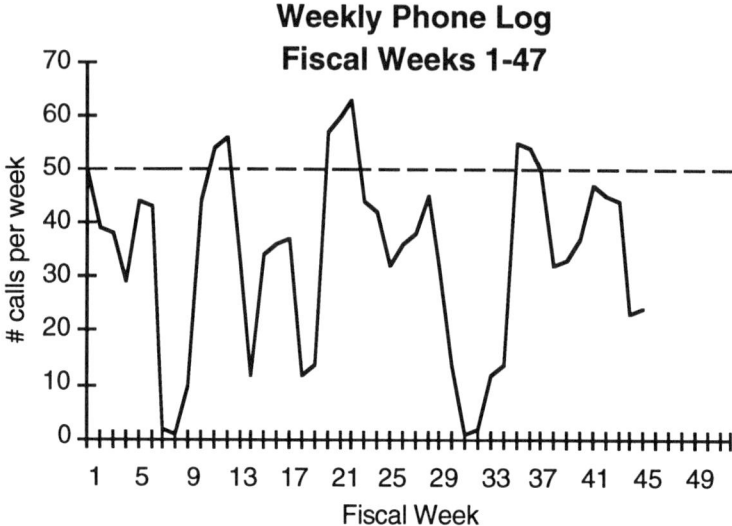

Figure 8.5: Weekly Phone Log

Figure 8.5 is a graphical display of the number of phone calls this salesperson made each week during 1996. This type of visual display is a very motivating way to see your progress over time. In the same way that setting weekly goals and daily targets gives you a small dose of positive reinforcement, this chart helps keep that going from week to week. If you see the trend begin to fall, it will motivate you to get it back up. If the trend is up, you will want to keep it that way. For the really brave at heart, you can double the impact by scheduling five minutes at the end of each month to review this chart with a friend, colleague, or your sales manager.

The style of chart in figure 8.5 is a good way to display data where you are primarily concerned with a weekly count. Sometimes it is more motivational to track the overall number for the month or year as in figure 8.6.

This style of chart shows overall progress, and it makes immediately obvious how you are doing against long-term goals. This "accumulated effort" chart is excellent for tracking results goals like number of sales, sales volume, or total commissions.

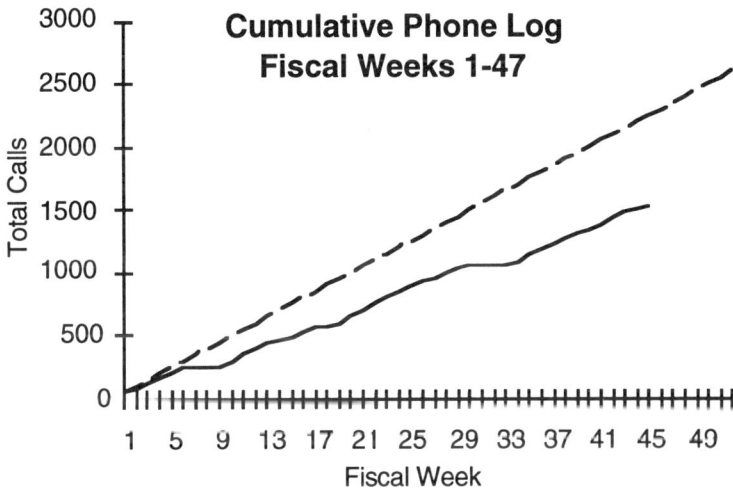

Figure 8.6: Cumulative Phone Log

I don't recommend making a graph for everything you are tracking. But for your most important activities (and results goals) it can be extremely valuable. Graphics are powerful because they add motivation for you and they make it easy to communicate your progress to others.

The most difficult challenge faced by any activity-based salesperson is maintaining consistent, moment-to-moment motivation. We said that it isn't enough to just remind ourselves that daily activities are connected to long-term goals, we have to find rewards for the activities themselves. The small feeling of satisfaction you get when you move a step closer to your goals is the positive reinforcement, or "mental fish," needed to maintain consistent motivation. Remember that much, if not all, of what we do is driven by what gets reinforced. Unlike animals, our most powerful rewards occur between our ears. Tracking is a tool to provide the mental fish that lead to the consistent motivation which ultimately leads to the success we seek.

Q&A:

Q: Don't you have to be anal retentive to track all this stuff?

A: No ... but it helps. It's certainly true that some personality types will find it easier to keep the detailed records necessary to benefit from tracking. And those who are more retentive (I include myself in this group) may track more items than those who are less retentive. But the motivational value is just as high for all personality types. Don't discount tracking just because you don't like keeping records. Try it for three weeks and see if it doesn't dramatically increase your activity and make it more fun.

Q: I already track my sales in reports to my manager. Isn't this enough?

A: Probably not. Remember, what we're trying to do here is use the principle of positive reinforcement to maintain your motivation in the critical activities that ultimately make you successful. Tracking a results-oriented goal like sales is important. It is vital. And it's also vital that you track activity if you want to maximize meaningful activity. This is not something you do for your boss. It's something you do for you.

Q: If I share my activity tracking with my manager, I can see how it would give me an added incentive to follow through on my goals. But what if he begins to expect this, and wants to see my activity numbers regularly?

A: Well, it depends on how brave you are. If you have a good manager and you trust him or her, you might benefit from their expecting to see your numbers regularly. We all need someone to hold our feet to the fire every now and then. If you feel your manager would use the data against you, think twice before using him as a coach.

Q: This is all well and good, but I would feel hemmed in to be such a slave to the numbers. I like to operate more loosely, where I can be free and unfettered.

A: I certainly respect this feeling. At first glance, it may seem that tracking restricts freedom. And, I guess actually, it does. It restricts your freedom to do things other than those that are most important to selling. Sometimes "free and unfettered" is a euphemism for, "I only want to do what I feel like doing." If you can think of a way to generate the sales you need without executing your key sales activities at their appropriate levels, then by all means sell that way. But if you believe that sales are built through consistent execution of certain activities, why *not* keep an accurate record of those activities. As for limiting your freedom, you are never a slave to the numbers. You can always change the numbers if something more important comes up (i.e. a meeting with a valued client). The numbers are meant to serve you, not rule you.

Application Exercises:

1. Create and use a phone log, or other activity log, for the next 3 weeks. Keep weekly logs in a three-ring binder or file so you can analyze your data at the end of the month.

2. Set up a graphical display for one of your important sales activities. Post the graph on the wall next to your desk where you have to see it every day.

3. Keep a time log for at least one day. Go ahead, do this one. I promise it will be a *very interesting* experience. See if keeping a record of your time doesn't make you more disciplined and focused.

4. **Bonus Exercise** Tell someone what you are doing and ask them to review your numbers with you at the end of each week for the next three weeks. This is a scary exercise ... and one that could cause you to literally *triple* your activity level.

Suggested Reading:

Karen Pryor, *Don't Shoot the Dog*, (New York: Bantam Books, 1984).

Chapter 9
Discipline

"If you think you can turn your work ethic on and off at will, one day you will try to flick the 'on' switch and it might not respond."

-- Pat Riley

It was the start of the 1985-86 NBA basketball season. The L.A. Lakers had won the championship the year before and *Sports Illustrated* said they were perhaps, "the greatest basketball team of all time."

It is tradition that the NBA champions be presented their championship rings in their home opener the following season. The L.A. Forum was packed that night with 17,505 screaming fans, all enthusiastically showing their appreciation for last year's world-championship performance. The arena was dark, illuminated only by a thick shaft of light that shone down from the rafters and formed a puddle on the floor below. The light followed each man as he emerged from the tunnel and walked slowly to center court, where he was greeted with a handshake and presented his diamond studded NBA championship ring. Each player thrust his jeweled fist high above his head, allowing the diamonds and gold to sparkle brilliantly in the spotlight. The fans erupted in applause and cheers all over again.

Throughout this ceremony, the Lakers opponents for the night, the Cleveland Cavaliers, sat quietly watching. The Cavaliers finished 21st in a league of 23 teams that year, but in coach Pat Riley's words, "On that night, they kicked our championship butts. We motivated them even when we couldn't motivate ourselves."

After the game a reporter stopped one of the Lakers on his way to the locker room. When asked why the Lakers appeared so uninspired, why they only seemed to play hard after it became obvious that they could lose, the player responded simply, "See me in March." Meaning that he would save himself, and only give his very best at the end of the season when it really counted. When told of his players comment, Riley said in response, *"If you think you can turn your work ethic on and off at will, one day you will try to flick the 'on' switch and it might not respond."*

The Lakers did make it to the playoffs that year. They were down three games to one in the western conference finals against the Houston Rockets. It was game 5, do or die for the Lakers. The game was tied with one second left on the clock. Houston's small forward, Rodney Macray, inbounded the ball from half court. The ball went sailing through the air and was greeted by all 7 feet 4 inches of center Ralph Sampson's fully extended body, twisting in the air as the ball touched his hands. Sampson flicked the ball toward the goal over the outstretched arms of Kareem Abdul-Jabbar, just as the buzzer sounded. The ball hit the rim, bounced straight up in the air, and in Riley's words, "fell like a boulder, right through the net." Asked about the game later, Riley said, "Holding back during the regular season had put us out of playoff condition. *We were playing below our potential and it had become a habit."* If you think you can turn your work ethic on and off at will, one day you will try to flick the on switch and it might not respond.[1]

Work ethic, effort, discipline. Whatever you want to call it, it's not something you turn on and off at will. *A high level of discipline either permeates your entire life or it is non-existent.*

---

[1] Adapted from *The Winner Within* by Pat Riley.

As we look at discipline in this chapter, we will see a consistent theme emerge: if you want discipline in your sales career, you must practice in every area of your life. I've never seen anyone who was completely undisciplined in one area of their life and totally disciplined in another.

Discipline, What is It?

Like the word emotion, *discipline* is a simple word we have used all our lives. Yet if ten people were asked to define it, they would come up with ten different answers. The dictionary defines discipline as: "an area of study," "to scold or rebuke," and "to force order upon." Depending on the context, the word discipline has widely varied meanings. Within the context of Activity-Based Selling, I believe it has three relevant meanings.

Meaning #1: *Beginning a task when you don't feel like it.*

Here, discipline occurs in the context of a specific event or action. If you really don't feel like making phone calls today, if you are experiencing emotions of lethargy, overwhelm, or depression, you can apply discipline and pick up the phone *in spite* of the way you feel. Elbert Hubbard was describing this kind of discipline when he said the key to success is to,

"Do what you must do, when you must do it, whether you feel like it or not."

Most people aren't aware that they can feel one way and act another. But the fact is it's something we've all done from time to time. Think of the first time you spoke in public. If you're like me, you didn't *feel* like stepping in front of that audience. I had weak knees, sweaty palms, and an unsettled stomach. In no way was I feeling up to what I was about to do. But I did it anyway, *in spite of how I felt.* You can be in a situation where every fiber in your body tells you to do one thing, yet still decide to do something else. This is really the core meaning of discipline: the ability to stand face-to-face with something you consider uncomfortable or distasteful and act in spite of those feelings.

This type of discipline is most often applied when you arrive at a new task or behavior. If you have completed your paperwork and it's time to pick up the phone, you have "arrived" at the task of making phone calls. The instant immediately before you do, or don't, execute a desired behavior is critically important. As you sit in your office looking at the phone, sometimes, for any number of reasons, you *really* don't feel like dialing. You begin to run through a mental checklist of other things you could do. Applying discipline in this critical moment means washing that checklist from your mind, and picking up the phone regardless of how you feel.

Meaning #2: *Resisting the urge to leave a current task*

It also takes discipline to stick with a difficult task after you have begun. Sometimes I start a task, say preparing a proposal, but then don't finish it. I work on it for 20-30 minutes, and then suddenly I am struck with an urge to do something else.

> Urge: a force or impulse that impels in an indicated direction.

In this case, the indicated direction is *away from* the current activity.

There is great danger here. Succumbing to these urges can kill activity just as much as never starting. When I looked back and analyzed why I was distracted I found there were two distinct types of urges that cause me to leave the tasks I was working on.

First, I am distracted by *internal urges*. I'm working on the proposal, when suddenly in my mind is the urge to get up, go to the bathroom, get a drink of water, or call a friend. Something *inside of me* has identified a more pleasurable alternative than what I'm currently doing. I have unknowingly been running through the mental checklist described above. When a more attractive activity is found, I am drawn to it. It is at this point that I must apply discipline to stay with what I am doing *in spite* of the urge to do something else.

The second class of urges that cause me to leave a current activity are *external urges*. Often when I'm working I will be distracted not by my own thoughts, but by something that comes *from outside of me:* a call from a friend, the mail being delivered, or a colleague walking into my office. If I am in the middle of a task that I don't like, there is a huge temptation to stop the task in favor of the interruption.

Now, I know what you're thinking, you *have* to take the call from a friend, and you *have* to talk with a colleague who walks into your office. You can't just ignore them. Well ... maybe. If you were getting paid $1,000,000 to complete the current activity within the next hour, could you tell your friend you'll call back? Ask a colleague to come again later? It *is* possible to resist the urge to be sidetracked by external distractions. Of course you have to use your judgement to know what's best in these situations, but if you choose, you can use discipline to resist urges generated by external distractions.

Meaning #3: *Staying the course*

This third meaning is significantly different from the first two in that it does not occur in the context of a specific event. Staying the course means sticking with a specified plan of action over a long period of time, even when the results of that action are not obvious.

During his tenure as President, George Bush was criticized heavily for his unwillingness to step in and stimulate a sagging economy. Bush's contention was that we were doing all the right things, the results just weren't showing yet. In his speeches he often pleaded with his listeners for our need to "stay the course," to stick with the current plan long enough to see the results. Because he lost the 1992 election, we'll never know if Bush was right, but his words provide a good illustration of the third definition of discipline relevant to Activity-Based Selling: to consistently execute a series of activities, over a long period of time, even if the results of those activities are not yet apparent.

Writing a book is a good example of a project that requires staying the course. Authors spend anywhere from six months to five years or more preparing a manuscript, in many cases not knowing if it will ever be published. Activity-based salespeople face a similar challenge every time they try a new marketing strategy or enter a new target market.

Used Sparingly, Discipline is a Great Motivational Tool

It may seem strange to devote a whole chapter to discipline when we said in chapter 2 that it is the motivational technique we *don't* want to rely on. We said that it was like trying to break through a brick wall instead of finding ways over, under, or around it. And while it's true that discipline is not the one and only tool we want to use to get ourselves into action, it does have an important place in the activity-based salesperson's motivational toolbox.

The truth is, we can't get along without discipline. Without it we would never do anything we didn't want to do or see any difficult task through to completion. It becomes a problem only when we rely on it as our sole behavior management tool. You can't just keep forcing yourself to do things you hate. Used this way, discipline rapidly becomes a hollow and shallow motivator. Used this way, it *is* like beating your head against a brick wall. You have to identify and solve the underlying problems causing you to hate a given task if you want *long term, consistent* motivation.

However, if you're not looking for long term motivation, discipline may be a good tool to consider. It's best when used in short spurts. Its value is not as a primary motivator for the normal work day, but as an *igniter* for normal, ongoing sales activities and as *fuel* for unique, non-recurring activities.

Suppose on a scale of 1-10 you rated your dislike for a certain activity at a 10+. If you use techniques like visualization, emotional control, or tracking, you should be able to reduce your negative feelings toward the task from a 10 to a 7 or 6 or even a 5. But still, it's not always that appealing to get started on something you hate at a level

5. Even with the other techniques we've covered in this book, you still need discipline. In the brief moment of starting a new task, you may still need the ability to begin the task *in spite* of how you feel about it. Used as an *igniter* discipline helps overcome the "ignition anxiety" we all experience when beginning tasks we don't like. Here, discipline is used in a short spurt to fight off negative feelings toward a specific task. If those feelings resurface *during* the task, you can use a spurt of discipline to get back on track and rekindle your motivation.

Sometimes discipline can be used not just as the initial spark, but as the *fuel* needed to get through the entire task. Discipline is a process of "throwing off," or fighting through negative feelings. As such, it takes great energy. Far too much energy to use it as our prime motivator for normal recurring activities. But from time to time all of us have unique non-recurring tasks on our to-do list: a letter to the home office, the once a year sales report, or a special request from a client. If these tasks are relatively short, you may not want to use the more elaborate techniques we've discussed. It's probably easier and requires less energy to just push through the task, even if you dislike it all the way. It may take less time to just do it, to blast through it, than to investigate and remove the source of your discomfort. However, beware the temptation to use discipline all the time. Table 9.1 suggests some of its appropriate uses.

In summary, we've said that a high level of discipline is not something you turn on and off at will. It's either present in every area of your life or it's non-existent. We identified three meanings relevant to activity-based sales: the ability to get started, the ability to stick with a tough task, and the ability to stay the course. And we said that although it is not to be used as a prime motivator, it does have its place in the activity-based salesperson's motivational toolbox. One key issue remains: can discipline be developed? And if so, how?

Developing Discipline

Discipline *is* a skill that can be developed. Just because you haven't exhibited a high level of discipline in the past doesn't mean

> **Table 9.1: When to Use Discipline**
>
> | Use Discipline: | Find Another Motivator For: |
> |---|---|
> | As an igniter when getting started on ...
 ... making calls
 ... paperwork
 ... other regularly recurring activities | Getting through ...
 ... 20 hours of phone calls each week
 ... 10 hours of paperwork per week
 ... any regularly recurring sales activity |
> | As a spark to rekindle motivation if you feel the urge to leave ...
 ... phone calls
 ... paperwork
 ... other recurring activities | |
> | As fuel for ...
 ... a letter to the home office
 ... doing a special proposal
 ... responding to a unique request from a client
 ... other short, non-recurring activities | |

you can't in the future. Sometimes you'll hear one person say about another, "He has great discipline." In essence saying "They have it, I don't." But your level of discipline and self-control isn't something you're born with. It's not a permanent physical attribute like your height, color of your eyes, or bone structure. It's more like a moldable physical attribute: how much you weigh, your resting heart rate, your muscle tone. With some effort, you can develop discipline the same way you would develop any other muscle.

You already have some level of discipline. If you didn't your life wouldn't be working at all. And still, for almost everyone, developing an increased level of discipline will greatly enhance their professional and personal life. The following are three key development strategies, along with specific application ideas, for enhancing your current level of discipline.

Development Strategy #1: *Learn to recognize discipline opportunities*

The first key to using discipline is to remember, in the midst of everything else going on around you, that your actions are not governed by your feelings, that you can use discipline to get yourself into action. Remembering that discipline is available to you when you need it is the first step in using it. Unfortunately, this is not always as easy as it might sound.

I was working in my home office one Saturday morning. I had just finished some client paperwork and the next task on my to-do list was paying the bills. When I saw this, I immediately had a great sense that I didn't want to pay the bills. I thought of all the other things I could do, and felt sorry for myself for having to work on a Saturday. I convinced myself that it was unfair and decided to pay the bills later. Just as I was about to get up and walk away from the desk, I remembered this thing called discipline. I remember thinking that discipline is what you use to get yourself into action when you don't feel like getting into action. I decided to give it a try. I felt a strong urge to walk away from the desk, but told myself I didn't have to act on that urge. And then, side by side with my intense desire not to pay the bills ... *I began paying the bills*. What an incredible feeling of control. Once I started, and stopped focusing on how much I didn't want to pay the bills, I got caught up in the task and before I knew it I was done. It was a great success story of discipline, but it all began with my recognizing, *at exactly the right moment*, that I could use discipline in this situation.

If you are ever to reap the full benefits of discipline, you've got to remember to use it when you need it. To increase your chance of recognizing discipline opportunities ...

Identify Opportunities Up Front

When you're caught up in the flow of the day, it's not always easy to step back and analyze everything you're doing. It's not always easy to look and find places to apply the behavior management tools we've discussed in this book. It's much easier to identify potential uses up front.

With respect to using discipline in your daily work life, take a few minutes now, or after you finish this chapter, to identify areas where discipline could help you. Use table 9.1 to stimulate your thinking. Your answer might include things like: getting started on phone calls, plowing through the XYZ proposal, or sticking with the paperwork you hate so much. Jot your answers down on the back of a business card and carry the card in your pocket during the day, glancing at it from time to time.

Remember, you are trying to ensure that you don't forget about this valuable tool for short term motivation. Anything you can do to remind yourself is helpful.

Identify Potential Lag Times

To achieve great things, in sales or in life, requires sufficient faith to endure "lag time." Lag time is the time between when you begin a new project and when you see the results of your efforts. Cutting the grass is a good example of a project that provides immediate positive feedback. You can look behind you and see neat rows of freshly cut grass. Every step you take shows clear progress. The feedback is not so immediate if, instead of cutting, you are planting. After you spread and cover the seed you have to work every day to keep the new seeds moist. For some varieties, you won't see germination for several weeks. Those several weeks are called *lag time*, the interval from effort to result. The life of an activity-based salesperson is often more like planting seeds than cutting grass. Some of this seed planting may include: entering a new market, selling a new product, or trying a new sales strategy.

Think back to the story about the dolphin and the principle of positive reinforcement from chapter 8. The dolphin kept swimming through the hoop because it kept getting rewarded with fish. Just as much as any animal, human beings require regular positive reinforcement to maintain motivation. And for positive reinforcement to be most effective, the reinforcer should come immediately after the desired behavior. But by definition, lag time means positive reinforcement is delayed. One of the fundamental motivators of human behavior is being withheld. It takes a significant amount of faith not to lose motivation during lag time.

If you want to "stay the course," it's helpful to identify potential lag times up front. If you're prepared for it, you won't be as disappointed when you don't see immediate results. Look at some of the activities you are working on now that are frustrating you. Is it possible that you're simply going through lag time? What about some of the new projects you are about to take on? Realistically, how long will it be before you see the results of your actions? It's interesting that most people underestimate lag time by 200-300%. Because they aren't prepared for how long they will have to wait, they give up just before they are about to see the fruits of their labor.

You can explore this issue further by asking someone you think of as highly successful to tell you about the early stages of their career, the trials and tribulations as well as the successes. You'll be amazed at what you hear. I was shocked when one of my mentors told me she had nearly starved for seven years before experiencing any measurable financial success. That could have been very disheartening, but instead it helped me to identify some of the potential lag times I would experience. I realized that the problems I was facing were a normal part of the success cycle.

No one wants to work hard for nothing. It can be very helpful to realize that in many cases your efforts *are* producing results, even if you can't see them yet.

Development Strategy #2: *Exercise the discipline muscle*

Just like learning to swing a golf club, the more you use

discipline the more comfortable you become with it. If you want to increase your comfort in using this motivational tool ...

Practice in small areas

In the same way you have to start small when building a muscle, you have to start small when developing discipline. You wouldn't ask someone who could only lift fifty pounds to lift a hundred. And you shouldn't expect yourself to apply large amounts of discipline until you've shown skill in applying small amounts.

Along the wall in most well-equipped gyms you will find a dumbbell rack. The rack is a narrow steel frame that stands about three feet high and holds sets of dumbbells arranged from smallest to largest. If you want to use the dumbbells, you simply walk over to the rack, scan all the choices you have, and pick up the set that is right for you. If you normally use the 20lb dumbbells, it would be insane for you to pick up the 85lb set and think you could do the same workout. I know. I've tried.

After reading this chapter, it might still be hard to discipline yourself to make two hours of phone calls, or do two hours of paperwork if you really hate those things. You need to start with a lighter weight. Find some smaller tasks you only moderately dislike and practice disciplining yourself to do them. You want to get comfortable with what it feels like to not want to do something, and then do it anyway. Think of the these tasks as "discipline dumbbells," and think of your goals or desires as a dumbbell rack. Scan the rack and choose a weight that is right for you at this point in your development.

One of the tasks I use for developing my own discipline is cracking the ice trays. As of the writing of this book, we don't have an automatic ice maker. We have five ice trays and a large bin which sits in the door of our freezer. When I go to the freezer and find the ice bin empty there is always the temptation to crack only one ice tray, take what I need, and let the rest of the family fend for themselves. When I'm in a hurry, or if I'm not feeling well, the temptation to crack only what I need is *extremely* large. Cracking ice trays is a small task I don't enjoy. And because it's a small task, it is an *ideal* exercise in discipline. When I go to the freezer and find the bin empty, I am standing face-to-face with a task I don't want to do. I don't want to do it, don't feel like doing it ... and, on a regular basis, *do it anyway*. It builds in me the confidence and strength to discipline myself to do bigger and scarier tasks. Because someday I want to be able to lift 85lb dumbbells, I begin with small ones.

Resist Other Urges

Salespeople are constantly required to resist the urge to do easier and more pleasurable tasks than the difficult but more important tasks they should do. They are also faced with the urge to leave an important task for something more comfortable. Because the process of resisting an urge is similar regardless of the subject of the urge, you can use other, non-work related temptations to practice and strengthen your resistance.

Think of some temptations you face regularly: smoking, drinking too much, or perhaps eating too much. I'm not asking you to give these things up altogether, but to resist the urge for a short time. Next time you would normally smoke, have a drink, or eat something that you shouldn't, delay it for 20-30 minutes and feel what it's like to resist an urge. Practice getting comfortable with that feeling.

Anything that urges you or draws you toward it is an ideal opportunity to practice discipline. And the more comfortable you become with feeling one way and acting another, the greater will be your power in using discipline in every area of your life, including creating sales activity.

Go the Extra Mile

The opportunities for practicing discipline are endless. One exercise I find particularly valuable is what I call "going the extra mile." It means pushing yourself beyond what's comfortable to accomplish more than you would have otherwise. Example: Next time you're doing something in the lawn (mowing, raking leaves, etc.) and you feel like quitting, push on for another 15-20 minutes. At work, when you meet your quota of phone calls for the day, push on and do 10% more. There are always avenues to practice the art of discipline if you look for them. And the more you practice, the more you'll be able to use "the big D" when you need it.

Visualize

We discussed visualization extensively in chapter 6. I mention it here to remind you that it can be used to practice *anything* you can do in real life, from driving a race car, to hitting a golf ball, to using discipline to get yourself into action.

In a quiet place, close your eyes and see yourself ready to begin a task you really dislike. Feel the internal feelings and urges you normally experience that would make you turn away from the task. Now, with that feeling still firmly in mind, see yourself *begin the task anyway*. Simultaneously feel the dislike of the task and see the action of doing the task. Repeat the affirmation, "My feelings don't control my actions. I do. My feelings don't control my actions. I do. My feelings don't control my actions. *I do.*"

All these discipline exercises are designed to build "muscle memory" for using discipline. If you play golf, you know what if feels like to make a good swing. If you're skilled at using discipline, you know what it *feels* like to do something even when you don't want to do it. Just keep in mind that practice is not an end in itself. You want to carry the ability to discipline yourself into the work place and use it to make calls, write letters, complete paperwork, and do all the other things needed for sales success.

Development Strategy #3: *Explore the feeling*

Anything you can do to heighten your awareness of what discipline feels like inside of you will be a great help in using this motivational tool. To increase your awareness ...

Discuss discipline with a friend

Take some time and share what you've learned in this chapter with a friend. Tell them what you agree with and what you don't. Share your definition of discipline and inquire about theirs. Describe, to the best of your ability, what it feels like inside to not feel like doing something and to do it anyway.

Write about discipline

Spend a half-hour committing to paper what you've learned about discipline. Record some of the key distinctions you've made and define areas where you are still unclear. Record in a few sentences your own definition of discipline. Describe how it feels to have an urge to do one thing yet do something else.

Beware Overuse

You don't want to have to use discipline too often. It's a dicey situation at best to get yourself to do something your mind is telling you you really don't want to do. Would you like to walk into the office every day really hating the thought of picking up the phone and having to discipline yourself to do it anyway? Or would you rather walk in looking forward to making the calls. Because discipline has such a powerful and immediate effect, once developed there is a tendency to overuse it. Rather than finding and removing motivational obstacles to regular tasks, you try to blow through them and ignore the underlying problem causing the pain. Discipline is not, I repeat is not, the preferred method of behavior management. It is extremely valuable in short bursts, but if used as your sole motivator, it will lose its effectiveness very quickly.

In this chapter we defined discipline as the ability to act in spite of mental barriers that make a particular task scary or uncomfortable. We said that discipline is not something you can turn on and off at will. A high level of discipline either permeates your life or it is non-existent. I gave you some ideas for how to start using discipline in the small areas of our life, because until you can exhibit discipline in the small areas, you'll never exhibit it in the large ones. Just remember, *"If you think you can turn your work ethic on and off at will, one day you'll try to flick the 'on' switch and it might not respond."*

Discipline is not the most comfortable behavior management strategy, but it is a valuable one to have in your motivational toolbox. Begin practicing some of the things we talked about and I can guarantee that as your discipline develops you will have a new sense of control and significantly improved results.

Q&A:

Q: Aren't some people just naturally more disciplined than others? Can I really *learn* to be more disciplined?

A: It depends on what you mean by the word "naturally." Certainly some of us experienced more discipline when we were growing up and therefore find it easier to discipline ourselves today. But as far as discipline being a genetic trait, I know of no data to support such a belief. Discipline is a learned skill. A great deal of our behavior is directed by feelings and urges we respond to without thinking. Discipline is simply the process of overriding these urges and taking conscious control of our behavior. Practicing discipline in small areas of your life helps you learn what it feels like to have an urge and not respond to it. By learning to not automatically act on your feelings, you are learning discipline.

Q: How does "exploring the feeling" help develop discipline?

A: Being good at discipline means being good at feeling one way and acting another. You need to be comfortable with knowing that you can override an urge when it strikes. Writing about how you feel or discussing it with a friend will increase your awareness and comfort with these feelings. As you understand that these urges are just feelings, not some irresistible force, you will be better at challenging them. After several years of studying and writing about discipline, when I find myself saying, "I don't feel like doing this," the words that come screaming into my head are, "Do it anyway." This is my way of reminding myself that if I choose to I can consciously direct my actions in spite of the way I feel.

Q: Why should I avoid using discipline as my primary motivational tool?

A: Remember, discipline is the most difficult form of behavior management. It generates the most stress. It is the process of getting yourself to do something *in spite of* the way you feel about it. The other motivational tools we've discussed change the way you think about a task so you actually *feel* like doing it. This generates much less stress and therefore is a much better long term motivational strategy. For most people, discipline is the only self-motivation tool they've ever known. Once they learn to maximize its effect, it's easy to fall into the trap of using it exclusively. While it is good for short term motivation, if you use discipline as your sole motivational tool, it will quickly lose its power.

Application Exercises:

1. Choose a task around the house that will serve as your primary discipline practice exercise (i.e. cracking ice trays, taking out the trash, paying bills, or whatever) From this day forward, every time you are faced with that task, discipline yourself to do it no matter how you feel. Notice what it is like to not feel like doing something and to do it anyway.

2. Identify the work activity that you find most difficult to stick with once you have begun (phone calls, proposals, applications, etc.). For the next week, every time you have an urge to leave this work activity, discipline yourself to keep going for another 15 minutes.

3. Have lunch with someone you consider to be very successful. Ask them to tell you about the early stages of their career, the trials and tribulations as well as the successes. Share the concept of "lag time" with them and see if they agree that lag time is a normal part of the success cycle.

Chapter 10
Miscellaneous Motivational Techniques

*"Never get so fascinated by the extraordinary
that you forget the ordinary."*

-- Magdeline Nabb

I store all my tools in the basement. I keep the bigger things: the power saw, the electric drill, and the electric sander in a cabinet; and smaller tools: wrenches, screwdrivers, and pliers in a nearby toolbox. Some tools are bigger and require more space. That's why I keep them in a cabinet. It's hard to fit a circular saw into a toolbox. Some are more complex and require several pages of instructions. Others have no instructions at all. You don't need a great deal of training to know how to use a hammer. *But the value of a tool is not determined by how big or complex it is* When you need a hammer, a hammer is much more effective than a circular saw.

The techniques for creating activity we will cover in this chapter are like the smaller tools I keep in the toolbox. These techniques don't require as much space or as many instructions, but they are *of no less value* than others we've devoted entire chapters to. As we wrap up this section on creating activity, I wouldn't feel it was complete if I didn't share with you several simple but powerful techniques I continue to use to manage my own motivation.

The Tools

In this chapter we will look at 6 new tools for self-motivation. They are in no particular order. Some are related to each other, some are not. The common thread is that all these techniques are designed to increase the level and effectiveness of your sales activity. Here's what we'll cover:

1. Managing Internal Dialogue
2. Turning Work into "Flow"
3. Repetitive Reading
4. Visual Reminders
5. Using a "Conditioning Book"
6. Public Commitment as a Motivational Tool

Technique #1: *Managing Internal Dialogue*

We all have thoughts and ideas racing through our minds every minute of every day. When these thoughts are represented verbally (as opposed to visually), we call them "internal dialogue." Internal dialogue goes on all the time. Unless you consciously focus on it, you probably aren't aware of it, but it's happening none the less. For example, if you were solving a crossword puzzle your internal dialogue might go something like this, "One across ... Slang term for diamonds? ... hmm ... Slang term for diamonds? ... (with excitement) Rock! A diamond is a *rock!* ... No, only three letters ... three letters, diamond, slang term for diamond ... three letters ... (long pause) ... (with a great sense of victory) *of course* ... ice." This is just one example of how we use internal dialogue. It comes from the same portion of the brain as speech, we just don't say the words out loud.

In addition to being used to solve problems, we are constantly using internal dialogue to make commentary on our performance and, even more dangerous, on our value as a person. Suppose you are a person who has a habit of being consistently late for appointments. Each time you arrive late a voice inside your head says, "Damn, late again. Why can't I be on time? What's *wrong with me?*" Your commentary has generalized this one event into a question about your self-worth. Suddenly being late has gone from a simple behavior problem to being something "wrong" with you. This kind of dialogue goes on all the time and it is incredibly damaging to self-esteem. With all the pain and rejection involved in Activity-Based Selling, I don't think I need to explain why low self-esteem leads to low activity.

To manage internal dialogue we have to take conscious control of the otherwise free-wheeling voices that churn inside our heads. There are two times it's particularly important to do this. The first is when you are commenting on a current or past situation. For example, suppose a person regularly misplaces their car keys and ends up running around in a frenzied panic every morning looking for them. In a state of anger and frustration they might say, "#@%&$*#@%! I'm *always* losing my keys. Why can't I keep track of things?" This dialogue has at least three major problems.

1. **First,** by saying over and over again, "I always lose my keys," you are conditioning yourself to continue to lose your keys. I don't pretend to fully understand how the subconscious mind works, but I can see no benefit from giving it instructions to do the very thing you are trying to avoid.

2. **Second,** this dialogue will exacerbate emotions which are already on edge. A statement like, "I always lose my keys," is a gross generalization. If it were indeed true that you *always* lost your keys, that you *never* put them down and remembered where they were, this might be something to be upset about, but that's not what happened. You simply misplaced your keys on this particular occasion. By saying, "I *always* lose my keys," you have used a generalization to make the situation seem much worse than it really is. And this generalization will tend to inflame rather than subdue your emotions.

3. **And third,** the question, "Why can't I keep track of things?" carries with it the implicit answer, "Because there's something *wrong with me*. I'm somehow flawed and it's showing up in my inability to remember where I put things." If you ask yourself enough of these questions and have enough implicit answers like this, your self-esteem will most certainly be eroded.

A better strategy when commenting about things that happened in the past is to force yourself to be 100% objective. Don't say, "I always lose my keys," but instead, "I misplaced my keys today." The first statement is a generalization; the second is an accurate statement based on actual data. Accurate statements are always better than inaccurate ones. The most common problem people face when thinking about past events is that they over generalize. Even if you have lost your keys every day for the past three weeks, it's not accurate to say, "I *always* lose my keys." The accurate commentary would be, "I've lost my keys every day for three weeks." The best advice I've ever heard regarding internal (and external) dialogue is, *"Never say anything you do not wish to be true."* It's a good rule of thumb to follow.

The second instance in which it's particularly important to take conscious control of your internal dialogue is when you are making commentary about the future. In thinking about the future, we often say things like, "Don't forget to ask for referrals before you leave." or, "Don't lose your keys again." Internal dialogue generates images based on the words we choose. If you say, "Don't lose your keys again," chances are the image that comes to mind is *losing your keys* (i.e. a picture of yourself absentmindedly putting the keys in a place you will never find them; or a picture of yourself running around frantically looking for them.) By playing these images in your mind, you are unknowingly performing *negative* mental rehearsal. You are actually rehearsing the behavior you are trying to avoid.

When thinking about the future it's better to think about what you want to happen rather than what you want *not* to happen. You want your words to generate images of your desired behavior rather than the behavior you are trying to avoid. The simplest way to do this is to keep your internal dialogue positive. "Always remember to ask for referrals," and, "Always remember your keys," are better internal statements than, "Don't forget to ask for referrals," and, "Don't lose your keys again."

All the adjustments to thought processes we've talked about in this book require one key element, that you be *aware* of what's going on in order to take steps to change it. Managing internal dialogue is no different. Here are four specific times you can use internal dialogue to your benefit:

1. **When you happen to be aware** of your internal dialogue, manage it carefully. Make sure you are making objective commentary instead of generalizations. When you think about the future, keep your words positive, generating images of your desired rather than undesired behavior.

2. **When you find yourself in an emotional tizzy**, if you can remember, check your internal dialogue. When you are highly emotional it is particularly important to stay objective and accurate about what has actually occurred. Don't make gross generalizations (thereby attacking your self-worth) for what is actually a discrete event.

3. **When you have a specific behavior** you want to change, practice the internal dialogue you would like to have in advance. See yourself in the situation and practice positive, objective comments. This will heighten your awareness and enhance the chance of your producing positive dialogue in the actual situation.

4. **When you are speaking aloud,** apply the same rules we've talked about regarding internal dialogue. One of the best ways to avoid making generalizations inside your head is to stop making them outside your head.

Technique #2: *Turning Work Into "Flow"*

The best way to be successful as an activity-based salesperson is to enjoy the work you do, *not* for the promise of some distant reward, but for the sheer pleasure of doing the work. If you don't enjoy it, the repetitive nature of your work is sure to make it seem tedious and boring. Most of us have experienced at least a few times when our work has been incredibly engaging and motivating, when we were so consumed with the task at hand that we became unaware of the world around us. This total absorption is what author Mihaly Csikszentmihalyi calls "Flow," an all consuming but pleasant obsession that appears randomly and lasts for moments, sometimes hours, then departs as mysteriously as it came. But this state of absorption doesn't have to happen by chance. There are specific ingredients that combine to transform ordinary activities into Flow. If we know what these ingredients are, we can consciously make them part of our work, transforming it from tedium to stimulating and energizing Flow. In his book *Flow: The Psychology of Optimal Experience*, Csikszentmihalyi identifies the following as factors that turn ordinary tasks into Flow:

> **Challenge.** I have a friend who often says about repetitive tasks, "If I know I can do something, I'm not motivated by it. I need to be *on the edge.*" What he is saying is that if he is not challenged by the task, he would rather not do it. This "need to be on the edge" is something many of us face, and it can be tremendously damaging to effectiveness if your job involves a lot of repetitive activity. By taking what was a routine task and setting a huge, stretch goal, you can make the mundane seem challenging and exhilarating. If your normal daily quota for outbound calls is 10, for one day set a special goal of 50 or 100. If it normally takes you an hour to complete an

application, try to do it in 10 minutes. Not only will this make routine tasks challenging, but this kind of thinking often leads to innovative breakthroughs in the way you do your work.

Clear goals and immediate feedback. The clearer the goals and the more immediate the feedback, the more an activity seems like a game. This is why electronic video games are so absorbing: the goals are crystal clear and feedback is instantaneous. Though we will probably never make work seem like a video game, by defining small but precise goals with very short deadlines, we can approach the level of instantaneous feedback.

One way to set and track extremely short deadlines is to use an electronic egg timer. The idea is to see how much you can accomplish in a finite time frame, say 15-20 minutes. You can see how many phone calls you can make, or how quickly you can complete an application, or whatever. It may sound silly, but if you are serious about it, you'll soon find yourself so wrapped up in trying to beat the clock that you forget that you are working. I recommend timing things in increments no larger than 15 minutes. Remember, we're trying to create immediate feedback toward a clear goal. It wouldn't be much fun to say "I'll complete this report in the next sixteen hours." The feedback isn't immediate enough. A better goal statement would be, "I'll complete the first page of the report in the next fifteen minutes." Keep goals clear and deadlines short and your work will be much more fun.

Laser focus. Learn to work on one thing at a time with total concentration on the task at hand. Pretend that the rest of the world doesn't exist. This single-minded devotion to a task is what time management expert Alec MacKenzie calls, "single handling," and he says you can increase your effectiveness by as much as 50% in one day using this principle. If you can shut out all the things happening around you and have total focus on the task at hand you'll soon find yourself deeply engaged in a Flow experience.

> *"Genius is the ability to delete most of your experience."*
>
> -- *John Grinder*

A sense of control. When you set long-term goals, like selling a million dollars worth of product in a year, forces beyond your control can influence the outcome. You should definitely have long-term goals, but for the sake of making work Flow, set up tasks where you have *complete control* over the outcome. Not "I will sell one million dollars worth of product this year," but, "I'm going to make 5 calls in the next 15 minutes." The outcome of this smaller task is definitely within your control. Work activities are much more likely to become "Flow" when you have total control over the outcome.

Technique #3: *Motivation Through Repetitive Reading*

In chapter 6 we established that subtle thoughts have a powerful effect on behavior. If you start to feel a little tired while making phone calls and and the thought enters your mind, "It's okay to take a break," you will likely put down the phone and get a cup of coffee, chat with a colleague, or go to the bathroom. If however, when you feel a twinge of tiredness your subconscious returns the thought, "I persist until the job is complete ... *even when I'm tired,*" chances are you will keep dialing.

Repetitive reading is the practice of reading the same passage (a short poem, excerpt from book, etc.) again and again, over a period of weeks or months, for the purpose of conditioning desired thoughts and behaviors. Through sheer repetition, your mind is conditioned to return thoughts that are the focus of your reading. We usually read things to obtain information. Once we have the information, there is no value in reading it again. However, if our purpose is not to get information, but to condition attitudes and behaviors, reading the same passage again and again can be of *great* value.

There are an almost infinite number of sources for this kind of material. Og Mandino's book, *The Greatest Salesman in the World*, is specifically designed for repetitive reading. If you haven't read this book, I highly recommend it. Even if you only read it once it will be a great inspiration, and if you read it over and over it could transform your life. The following is a passage from *The Greatest Salesman in the World:*

> I will persist until I succeed.
>
> The prizes of life are at the end of each journey, not near the beginning; and it is not given to me to know how many steps are necessary in order to reach my goal. Failure I may still encounter at the thousandth step, yet success hides behind the next bend in the road. Never will I know how close it lies unless I turn the corner.
>
> Always will I take another step. If that is of no avail I will take another, and yet another. In truth, one step at a time is not too difficult.
>
> I will persist until I succeed.

What would happen if you took on the attitudes and behaviors described in that passage? You really don't need any sophisticated technique to condition these attitudes, just spend a few minutes each day reading this kind of material and it *will* impact your behavior.

Another of Mandino's books, *Mission Success*, contains a short section called "The Seeds of Success" that is designed to be read everyday. I have used this passage for my own motivation for many years, and probably will for the rest of my life. James Allen's small book, *As A Man Thinketh*, is so short and powerful that the entire book could be used for a repetitive reading exercise.

When you begin looking, you'll find things you could use for repetitive reading everywhere: magazine articles, a favorite poem, a passage from a book, or even the lyrics to a song. Choose anything that inspires you, and make sure that it is conditioning habits and beliefs that you want to incorporate into your behavior. If you need persistence, read passages that inspire you to persist and it will be reflected in your behavior.

Repetitive reading is amazingly simple and powerful. Give it a try. Read the same inspiring text every day for three weeks and I *guarantee* you will witness a marked improvement in your behavior, attitude, and performance.

Technique #4: *Visual Reminders*

Visual reminders are things you place in your environment to remind you of new behaviors you want to create. They can be signs you place in your car, in your date book, or by your desk. They can even take the form of "cue cards," notes to yourself written on index cards that you carry in your pocket and look at throughout the day. The basic idea is to capture on paper something you want to be reminded of regularly and then put that reminder in a place where you will stumble across it several times a day.

One of the attitudes I've tried to condition into my subconscious is what I call a "bias toward action." I know that the two keys to success are the ability to create a good plan and the ability to consistently execute that plan. Either one without the other is of little value. I'm a very introspective person. I'm very willing to sit quietly and plan a project, a sales call, or even a vacation. But sometimes I think too much and don't *do* enough. I get "paralysis by analysis." One day while sitting at my desk thinking about my paralysis problem, two phrases jumped into my mind. They were very simple, but had great emotional power for me. Every time I thought of them I was inspired to stop thinking and start *doing*. I made signs with these two phrases and posted them near my desk. They were handwritten on notebook paper with a thick marking pen. The signs said,

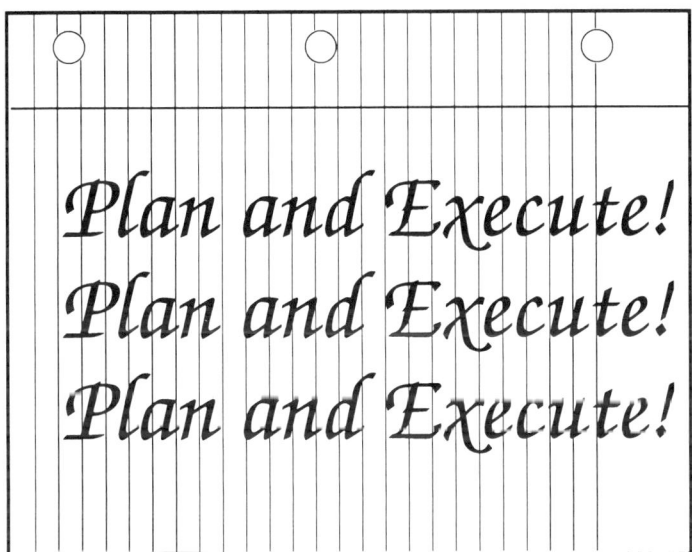

These sets of words had significant motivational value for me. I would read them every morning and several times throughout the day and I was reminded of my need to get on with it, to execute, to *do* something. This focus on execution reduced my tendency to over plan and significantly increased my productivity. Everyone who came by my desk thought I was a little weird, but I didn't care. At least they knew I was serious about making things happen, and they probably walked away thinking about their own level of commitment and motivation.

I'm not sure why, but these two phrases still have a great deal of emotional power for me. Maybe because these words perfectly captured the emotions I felt when they first popped into my mind. Whatever the reason, they have been great inspirations for me for many years now. I still have the original signs I wrote that day.

As you can see, the structure of visual reminders is very flexible. The central idea is to place in your environment visual cues that will force the repetition required for subconscious imprinting. To get maximum benefit, find phrases or pictures that grab your emotions. The more often you see them and the stronger the emotions they elicit, the more powerful an impact they will have.

Technique #5: *Using a Conditioning Book*

Have you ever had a spark of great inspiration? At one time or another we have all listened to a tape, read a book, or heard a speaker who made us feel like we could do anything. Wouldn't it be great if you could feel that way every day? What do you think feeling that way on a *regular basis* would do to your activity level and your sales revenue? A "conditioning book" is a tool you can use to rekindle that inspiration every day.

A conditioning book is a collage of pictures, words, and phrases that inspire you. These words and images remind you of all the reasons why you want to excel in your chosen field. They remind you of the things about your job that excite and exhilarate you. They remind you that with effort and persistence all things are possible. By spending a few minutes every morning flipping through the pages of this book, you bathe your mind in positive, uplifting thoughts, rekindling the excitement and inspiration you need to excel in sales.

My conditioning book is a three ring binder with approximately 20 pages of words and pictures. When I find pictures that inspire me in magazines, catalogs, sales brochures, or wherever, I cut them out and put them in the book. I have pictures of some of the top performers in my field (Zig Ziglar, Earl Nightingale, Napoleon Hill), and of products I would like to produce (books, videos, and audio tape albums). The book also includes quotes, short excerpts from books, and ideas of my own. Sometimes when I have an idea that is particularly inspiring I'll jot down a few sentences to capture it and include these in the book. Listed below are some of the ideas I've included in my conditioning book which are aimed at developing the habit of consistent sales activity. Please feel free to use these if you find them inspiring.

"You may not be able to choose what you think or feel, but you can always choose what you do. Act and thoughts and feelings will follow."

-- Oz Garcia

"Learn to love the process more than the outcome."

-- Russ Merck

"We are what we repeatedly do. Excellence then is not an act, but a habit."

-- Aristotle

"Some planning and some action is better than perfect planning and no action. Once you decide to do something, don't look back, just do it!"

-- Russ Merck

> *"The things that you believe and the actions you take every day are what are going to determine your destiny."*
>
> *-- Anthony Robbins*

> *"I hold a doctrine, to which I owe not much, indeed, but all the little I ever had, namely that with ordinary talent and extraordinary perseverance, all things are attainable"*
>
> *-- T. F. Buxton*

I look through my book first thing in the morning to get me fired up for the day, and recently I've started taking a quick look at it in the afternoon. Because the afternoon is my low energy time of day, the conditioning book helps give me the motivation I need to push hard for the last few hours of the day. Don't feel you have to use it every day. I only use mine during the week, and if I miss a few days here and there I don't worry about it too much. The beneficial effects will be very noticeable even if you only use it 3 or 4 days a week.

The obvious benefit of using a conditioning book is that it will spark your short term motivation. And if that were all it did, it would be well worth the effort. But a conditioning book also has a subtle, long term effect that may be even more valuable than the short term motivation. After using your conditioning book for several months, you'll begin to notice small shifts in your attitude and behavior. You'll observe an increased determination in your actions. You may find yourself coming in earlier and staying later, not because you feel you have to, but because you *want* to. Little frustrations that used to bother you will become hardly noticeable. By continually bathing your mind with inspiring thoughts you can make a profound shift in attitudes and beliefs that will permeate your entire life. If you use the conditioning book long enough you *will* see this effect. And it is one of the most exciting things in the world to see your attitudes and behaviors naturally, effortlessly move in the direction you've chosen.

Technique #6: *Using Public Commitment as a Motivational Tool*

Several years ago I took a sales seminar that met once a week for eight weeks. At one point during the seminar I was very frustrated with my lack of consistent effort in making cold calls. During a break in the class that night I wrote out a simple one page contract stating that I would make 70 calls the next day. In the past I had been making 70-80 calls a *week*, so this was a huge stretch for me. Just to add a little more pressure, the contract stated that if I did not meet my goal, at the next class I would pay $10 to each class member and sing *God Bless America* a cappella. I signed the contract and gave it to the seminar leader who, to my surprise, made copies and distributed them to the entire class. As bad as it would have hurt to pay several hundred dollars to the class, that wasn't what motivated me most. I could never have lived down my off-key rendition of *God Bless America*. I had created *maximum* leverage.

Public commitment is the process of setting clear goals and then sharing them with others for the purpose of being held accountable. One of the great challenges of being an independent salesperson is that you are only accountable to yourself, and sometimes it's just too easy to let yourself off the hook. It's a fact of human nature that you'll work much harder to look good in front of others than you will if no one is watching. Public commitment puts this fact of human nature to good use.

Public commitment can take many forms. What I do today is set specific weekly goals for the level of all my key sales activities (calls, letters, and appointments), and then share those goals with at least one other person. For the past few years, every week I have faxed my goals to a good friend who lives in a different city. You can share your goals with your colleagues at the office, a friend far away (fax, e-mail), your spouse, or anyone else who is willing to help you. You can form a group of people who will meet and review their goals regularly. You can post your goals on the door of your office, or on your refrigerator at home. There's no end to the variations on this theme. Be creative and find a way that works for you.

After writing out the contract in the seminar that night, I went home and slept uneasily. When the alarm sounded at 6:00am the following morning, I sat bolt upright in bed. I jumped to my feet, took a quick shower, said a brief prayer and was sitting at the phone at 7:59am. When the clock ticked eight o'clock I began to dial ... *and nothing happened.* There was no dial tone. There were no tones from the buttons. The phone was completely dead. Scenes of me singing to a room filled with laughing people holding my money began to race through my mind. After trying the phone three or four more times, I began to panic. I saw myself standing in the rain with a bucket full of quarters, making 70 calls from the pay phone at the local gas station. As the sweat pouring down my forehead began to intermingle with the tears from my eyes, I tried the phone one last time ... and it worked. I don't know why, it just started working. I spent six straight hours doing nothing but dialing the phone. When I was done I had made 75 calls, spoken with 22 decision makers, and scheduled 7 appointments. It turned out to be one of the most productive days in my sales career.

Is public commitment a tough, scary way to motivate yourself? You bet it is. Is it effective? *Definitely.* If you want to get maximum impact from this powerful technique, here are a few tips.

Always make commitments in writing. Aside from making it easier for others to remember and track your goals, the process of writing helps the goals seem more tangible and concrete to you.

Choose someone you trust to share your goals with. It's best to have someone who cares about you and is willing to encourage you along the way rather than just check on you at the end. Whoever you choose should know why you are sharing your goals with them and be willing to help.

Share your goals with someone you respect a great deal. The more you respect the person with whom you share your goals, the less you will want them to see you falling short of what you said you would do.

Add additional leverage. If the prospect of appearing lazy or undisciplined in the eyes of another person is not motivation enough, add more leverage. Write your partner a check and tell them to cash it if you don't meet your goals. Or try the *God Bless America* approach. It worked for me.

In whatever form you choose, public commitment is a great motivator. It takes some courage, so start small and build up. Give it a try and find out how powerful this simple motivator can be.

I hope you find these six motivational techniques as valuable as I have. Combined with the other larger techniques we've discussed: energy management, mental imaging, managing negative emotions, tracking, and discipline; you now have an arsenal of skills to create high levels of activity.

However, we don't want to create activity just for the sake of activity. We want activity that produces results. In the next chapter we will discuss the five important changes you should consider making when working to refine the effectiveness of your activity.

Part III:
Refining Activity

Chapter 11
Assessing the Impact of Your Activity

"It is best to learn as we go, rather than to go as we have learned."

-- Leslie Jeanne Sahler

We don't want activity for the sake of activity, we want activity that achieves results. I was doing a seminar in London when one of the participants said, with regard to ensuring that his staff's activity was effective, "We don't want to be *busy fools*." I couldn't agree more. Life is too short to invest any of our efforts in ineffective activity. The last thing any of us want to be is a "busy fool." Up to this point, this entire book has been about how to define and produce significant sales activity. But at some point we have to stop and assess whether our activity is taking us in the direction we want to go. If we are not creating the results we want, then we have to stop and consider what adjustments we should make to our activity so that it will yield the results we want. The purpose of this chapter is to give you some *strategies for change* you should consider when evaluating the effectiveness of your activity. As you look to refine your activity, consider doing one or more of the following:

- Nothing
- Increase Your Activity Levels
- Increase Your Effectiveness Ratios
- Change Your Target Markets
- Change Your Sales Strategy

176 • Activity-Based Selling

Change Nothing

When you look back on the results you've produced over the past few months, even if you haven't done as well as you had hoped, consider the possibility that you may be doing everything right and that you simply need more time. Take a look at figure 11.1. If everything is on course and you are tracking according to plan, then it makes perfect sense not to make any changes. But what if you aren't on target? What if your results are more like those in figure 11.2, tracking well below plan? In this case you definitely need to change something, right? The answer is, *maybe*. I say maybe because it is possible you are doing everything right, but experiencing a phenomenon we discussed in chapter 9 called "lag time."

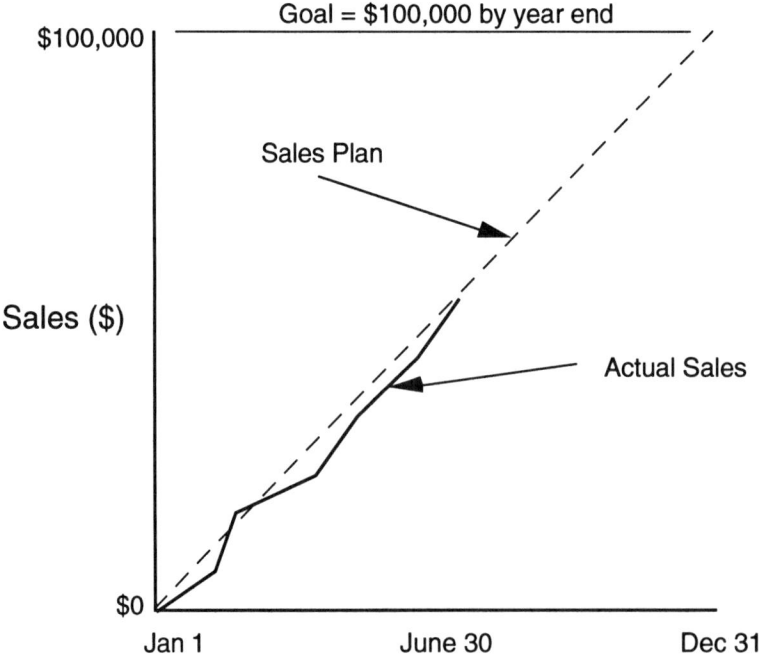

Figure 11.1   On Plan

Assessing the Impact of Your Activity • 177

Lag time is the delay between the time you start a new undertaking and the time results begin to appear. If you have recently entered a new market or begun a new sales strategy, you will probably experience some lag time in the beginning.

In many cases the reason for the delay between effort and results is obvious. If you begin a direct mail campaign, you don't expect results the first day. If you begin a new exercise program or plant a garden, you expect to have to wait to see results. However, in some new undertakings the reason for lag time is not so obvious.

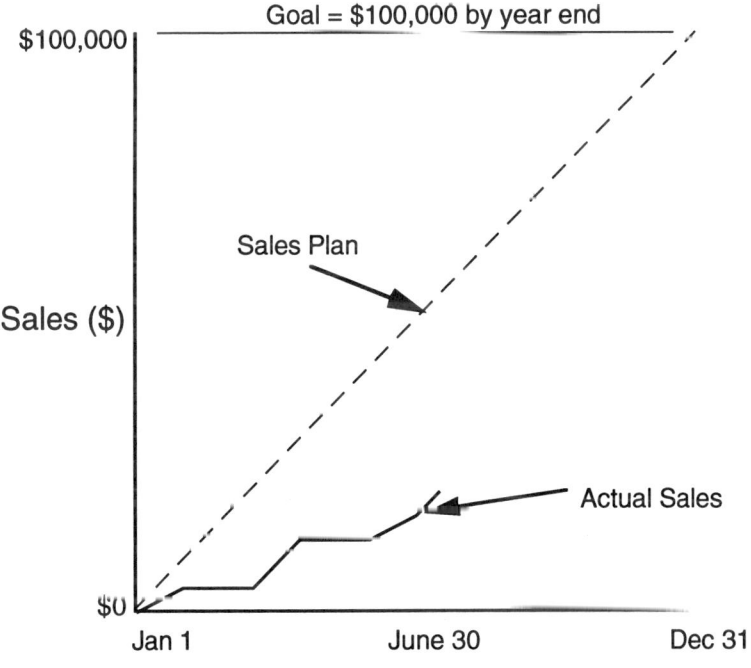

Figure 11.2   Tracking Below Plan

I remember selling tickets to my first public seminar. It was a seminar on time management and I was promoting it to local businesses. I worked for two weeks identifying prospects, making cold calls, having face-to-face meetings, and still didn't make a single sale. I was ready to give up when I shared my frustrations with a friend. I told him all I'd done over the past weeks and that I couldn't understand why I hadn't sold anything. He listened carefully and then said, "Russ, *don't change anything*. You're doing everything right. You're just in *lag time*." That was the first time I'd heard the term. He was so convincing that I decided to give it another week. I don't know if he was a prophet or just lucky, but over the next two days I sold 12 tickets. There was *no obvious reason* why people should be buying from me now, but for some reason they were.

If you've just entered a new market or implemented a new sales strategy, even if things aren't tracking according to plan, consider the possibility that you are doing everything right. We live in a world that celebrates immediate gratification: microwave ovens, cellular phones and ATM machines. We don't like to wait for anything. We have come to believe that success should come quickly, and if it doesn't, something must be wrong. But what a tragedy it would be to give up a sound sales strategy because you didn't believe in the success that was just around the corner.

Lag time is a phenomenon of new undertakings. If you are still selling the same way you've sold for years, and you are below your targets, chances are you need to make some changes. But new undertakings, breakthroughs, or innovations will always require a certain element of faith. Sometimes you have to put a lot of work into a garden before you see the little green plants peeking up through the surface. And sometimes it takes longer than what you think is reasonable. But you keep watering and waiting because you have *faith* that eventually the results will appear.

If your results are not what you'd hoped for, ask yourself the following questions to determine whether you are experiencing lag time.

Have you done all the right things? Suppose you are trying to penetrate a new market but after several months you've still not made a single sale. If you've done all the right things (identified the right prospects, mailed the right letters, and made the right calls), you are probably in lag time. How do you know if you've done the right things? By checking with someone else who has been successful at penetrating the same market.

Have others experienced similar lag times? If you're trying a new strategy or entering a new market and you know others who have tried similar things and experienced similar lag times, you are probably doing everything right and just need to be patient.

What does your intuition tell you? Sometimes things just feel right, and sometimes they don't. I can't give you a quantitative criteria for what "feels" right, but intuition can be a valuable guide. If it feels like you are doing all the right things and success is just around the corner, it probably is.

After you break through lag time, your results will begin to reflect your efforts. Your results will improve, and as in figure 11.3, you will begin to move toward your goals. If you've just begun a new approach or entered a new market, even if everything isn't on plan, be open to the possibility that you are doing everything right and that all you need is a little more time. All this discussion of lag time isn't meant to say that you don't keep looking for ways to improve, I just don't want you to get frustrated and turn your back on a sound strategy before it has time to begin bearing fruit.

Increase Activity Levels

If your results are not on plan, one of the first questions to ask yourself is, "Am I doing enough?" Maybe the answer is simply to increase the number of calls you are making, mail you are sending, or prospects you are seeing. If you are currently seeing 10 prospects a week and you increase that to 11, your sales should increase 10%. This is a pretty obvious one-to-one relationship between sales and activity. But I've noticed that there is a certain point where you begin to experience

180 • Activity-Based Selling

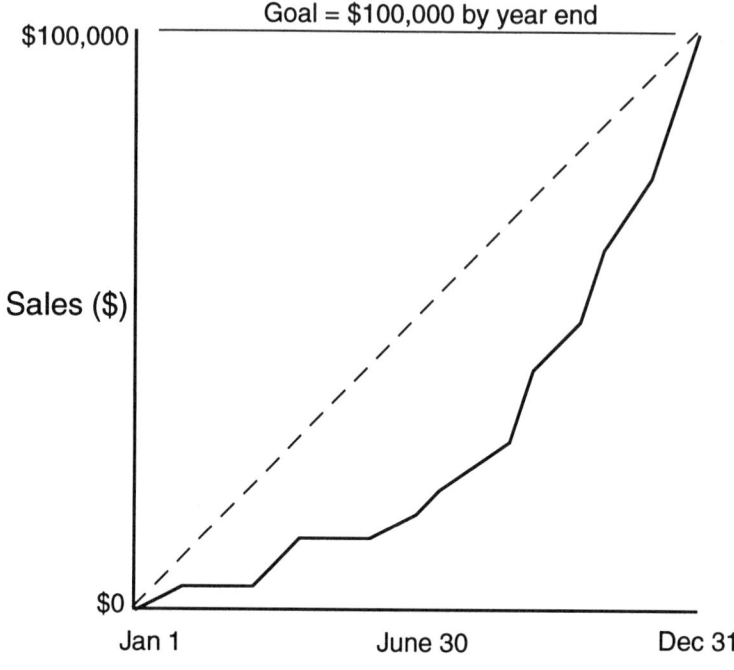

Figure 11.3   On Plan After Lag Time

a multiplier effect, a point where you increase activity by 10%, and sales increase 20 or 30 or even 40%. I call this reaching "critical mass."

The term "critical mass" comes from the field of physics. It is used to indicate the amount of radioactive compounds required to create a self-sustaining reaction. In business, critical mass can be thought of as the amount of effort or exposure needed before your efforts to begin to multiply on their own. When Cabbage Patch Dolls and Mighty Morphin Power Rangers became the rage, a large part of the marketing happened from one parent to another over the telephone or the backyard fence, or from child to parent in the form of a Christmas list. When they had achieved enough exposure, this word of mouth marketing kicked in and made these products the phenomena we know them as today. They had reached the threshold of exposure we call critical mass. For a retail product, critical mass is reached when product sales exceed approximately fifty million dollars a year. This is what author Dan Burris calls "product flash-point," where consumers switch from a passive interest to an attitude of "I have to have it." Examples from the last decade include: VCR's, CD players, and most recently cellular phones.

Fortunately, because most of us aren't selling a consumer product on a national scale, we don't have to sell fifty million dollars before things start rolling. But there is some level of activity required to experience this multiplier effect. Before you reach critical mass, every sale comes from your activity. You have to individually identify, contact, and persuade each prospect. Once you have achieved critical mass, things become easier. Now a significant portion of your business comes looking for you. In Activity-Based Selling, critical mass is the point where you are making enough calls, sending enough mail, and seeing enough prospects that people begin talking about you.

Critical mass can be generated by being in business for a long time. After 10-15 years, a real estate agent or insurance agent has touched enough people that there is a large constituency out there talking about him or her. Critical mass can also be generated by a high activity level. If you are only seeing 5 prospects a week, in a year you'll have touched 250 people. If you are seeing 20 people a week, after 12 months you'll have nearly over 1,000 people working for you as a silent referral source. If you are creating enough activity, people begin to hear about you from several different sources. You want them to say, "You know, you're the third person this week that has told me about Bob. Maybe I'll give him a call." The higher your activity level, the greater the chance those in your community will hear your name the 3-5 times required to move them to action.

In addition to a high activity level, consistency is also an important ingredient in creating critical mass. Early in my sales career I was a very inconsistent marketer. I kept thinking that I hadn't found the right sales presentation or the right target market. I was frustrated. Things didn't seem to be working for me like they were for others. I was questioning everything else when my problem was staring me in the face. I wasn't being consistent. My goal was to make 50 calls a week. Not a lot for some businesses, but for mine it's an aggressive target. Unfortunately, I didn't hit my target on a regular basis. Over the course of the year, many weeks I did make 50 calls, some weeks as many as 75, and others as low as 15, 10, or 0. I ended up with an average of just over 26 calls per week for the entire year.

I kept questioning my strategy, my presentation, and my target markets, but I wasn't being honest with myself. The truth was, for every 20 outbound marketing calls I made, I closed one sale. At my meager average of 26 calls a week I still managed to close 56 deals, a very respectable number. If I would have consistently hit my goal of 50 calls per week, I would have closed 125 sales, a phenomenal number. And 125 satisfied customers would have produced a lot more referrals and spin-off business than did the 56. If I would have pushed myself to 75 calls each week, a very reachable goal, I would have closed almost 200 sales, more business than I could have handled. I was lamenting the fact that my strategy wasn't working when indeed it was working. I just wasn't working it consistently enough. There were plenty of other salespeople who were doing better than I was even though their call-to-close ratio was poorer than mine. They were doing better because instead of complaining they were working and producing a lot more activity than I was.

In addition to the calls you are making, look at the other steps in your sales process, even if you don't have precise numbers. Think about the sales activities that are required to support the customer contacts you make. Are you doing enough prospecting, mailings, presenting enough proposals, and submitting enough applications to support the calls you are making and the people you are seeing? You may find as I did that you aren't spending enough time working on your prospect list. It's crazy, but many salespeople have a subconscious fear of depleting their prospect list, so rather than working hard to build it up, they just don't make calls. I guess that's one way to keep your prospect list full. Think about how much effort you are investing in each step in the entire sales process. If you aren't doing enough of these critical support activities, you may want to set a *time limit goal* (i.e., work three hours per week on your prospect list) for your most important support activities.

When looking to refine activity, one of the first questions you should ask is, "Am I doing enough? Do I have a strategy that is working and I'm just not working it hard enough or consistently enough?" To assess whether you are doing enough, ask yourself the following questions:

Does my activity level compare favorably to others in my industry? If you sell real estate and you only go on three sales calls a week, while the top performers are going on ten calls a week, you probably need to do more.

Do I put in enough hours? Sometimes an activity problem can be as simple as not putting in enough hours at the office. You may be working as hard (or harder) than the top performers, but if they get to the office at 6:30 and leave at 6:00 while you're only working eight to five, you can't hope to do as well as they are.

Am I being consistent enough? Do you make 100 calls some weeks and other weeks make none? Do you work extremely hard some weeks and others not hard at all. A consistent level of effort has many benefits. If there is significant variation in your activity level, you will probably greatly improve your production by making a more even, steady effort.

One of the difficulties with accurately assessing activity problems is that our ego often gets in the way. Because our self-esteem is closely tied to our behavior, we protect our view of ourselves by denying that we are doing less than we are capable of. Freud called this denial an "ego defense mechanism." We protect our ego by falsely believing we have done our best. While this ego defense mechanism may make us feel momentarily better, in the long run it is not healthy and does nothing to improve sales performance. Avoid falling into this trap by trying to view your sales process and your sales behavior with detached objectivity. Think of your behavior as an inanimate object, a machine that sometimes breaks and needs to be fixed. If your car has a flat tire, you stop and fix it. You don't continue to drive around on a flat tire pretending it's not there. If your sales machine isn't performing at optimal levels, don't hide from the truth, simply identify the problems and take steps to fix them. If your activity level hasn't been as high or as consistent as it should have been, that's okay, just turn up the fire and get yourself back on plan.

Effectiveness Ratios

One of the major benefits of keeping accurate records is that it allows you to clearly identify those steps in the sales process where you are not as effective as you could be. To refine your activity, you first need to decide which areas are in greatest need of improvement. What's more important: getting better at prospecting, preparing proposals, or honing your sales presentation? Ratio analysis helps answer this all important question.

Most salespeople are familiar with the terms *sales funnel* and *sales ratios*. "Sales funnel" is the name we give to the idea that the number of qualified prospects becomes continually smaller with each step in the sales process. "Sales ratios" are a measure of the number of prospects that fall out of the funnel after each step in the process. Figure 11.4 shows a typical sales funnel with its associated ratios.

Looking at figure 11.4, we see that for every twenty calls this salesperson makes, one person agrees to meet with him. For every ten interviews he conducts, he ends up submitting one proposal, and for every two proposals he submits, he closes one sale. This says that he consummates one sale for every 400 cold calls he makes. How do you know if these ratios are acceptable? There are lots of ways. The most obvious is to ask whether these ratios allow you to meet your sales goals. If you need to make 400 calls to close one sale, and you can only reasonably make 100 calls a week, that says you will close approx-

Assessing the Impact of Your Activity • 185

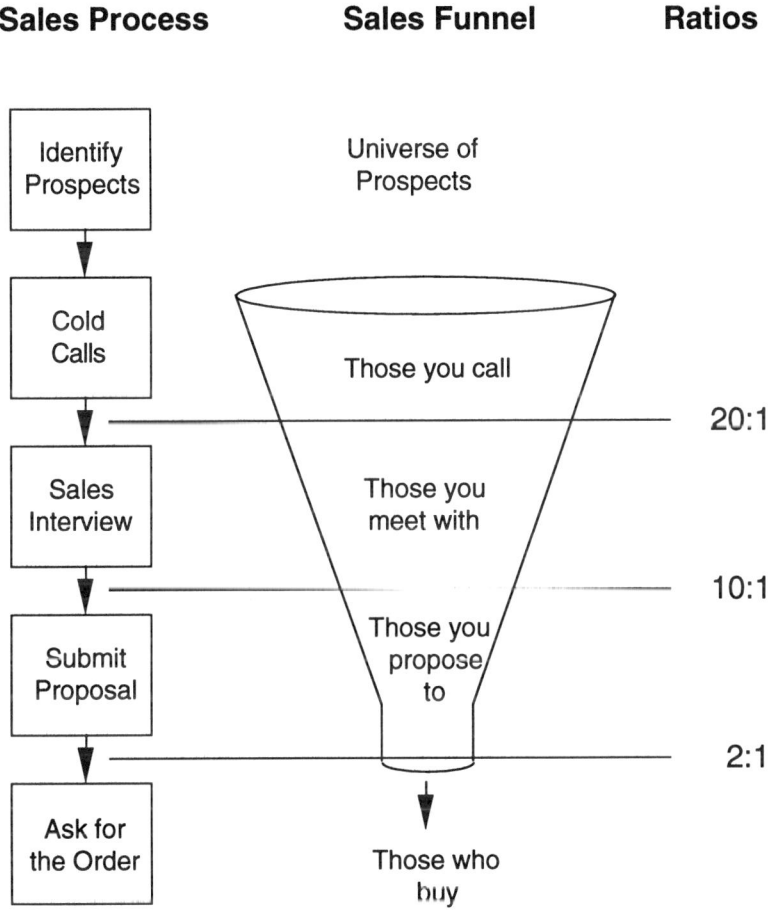

Figure 11.4 The Sales Funnel

imately one sale per month. Is that acceptable? It depends on the commission you make on each sale, but for most of us it wouldn't be nearly enough.

Suppose the example wasn't so obvious. Suppose your call-to-sale ratio was 100:1, about one sale per week. Is this good enough? Maybe. Perhaps that level of effectiveness has allowed you to reach your sales goals in the past. It's still a good idea to question specific ratios so you can target areas where you need to improve. One way to do this is to compare your ratios to someone else's. If you know someone who keeps impeccable records you can compare your ratios to theirs. Note that I said someone who keeps *impeccable* records. Beware the person who says, "Yea, I get about one meeting for every ten calls I make." People who don't keep accurate written records usually overestimate their effectiveness by at least 100%. It will be hard to find someone else who keeps good records because so few people do. If you can't find anyone, ask a buddy to start. You'll be doing him or her a big favor.

Aside from comparing your ratios to someone else's, use your own judgement to decide where you need to improve. You can look at your own numbers and say, "That interview-to-proposal ratio is really killing me. If I can find a better way to qualify prospects on the phone, my sales could double." Common sense should tell you that if only one person in 10 you meet with warrants a proposal, you aren't qualifying them well enough before you take the time to meet with them.

What you want to do is to target very precisely where you need to improve your sales *effectiveness*. For the call-to-meeting ratio, you would have to decide why it takes 20 calls to get one meeting. If we define a cold call as every time we dial the phone in an attempt to contact a decision maker, then there are several reasons why this ratio might be as high as it is. One reason might be that you aren't talking to decision makers when you call. Maybe you're calling at the wrong time to catch them in the office. Maybe you need a better strategy for getting past their secretary. Maybe the problem is that when you talk with them you can't convince them to meet with you. Using sales ratios to define problem areas helps you get to the highly detailed level of understanding where appropriate corrections can be made. Keeping highly detailed records is a prerequisite to getting the most from ratio analysis.

Six months into my first sales job I was struggling. I had sold almost nothing and had few prospects. Recognizing that I needed some help, I scheduled a meeting with a mentor and friend who was known as a sales guru. I began the meeting by telling him how tough things had been and that it didn't seem fair. I had been trying very hard and my results in no way reflected my efforts. He politely let me talk for a few minutes and then asked me a few simple but specific questions, "How many calls do you make each day? Of those calls, how many times do you speak with a decision maker? Of the decision makers you speak to, how many agree to meet with you? Of those you meet with, how many end up buying?" I hemmed and hawed for a few minutes and then sheepishly admitted I didn't know the exact numbers. I'll never forget what he said next. This friend and mentor, whom I respected more than words can express said, "Russ, *I can't help you if you don't know your numbers.*" He was trying to make a precise diagnosis of my sales problems, but without the data he was powerless to help me. That's when I began keeping precise records of everything I was doing. If you aren't currently doing this, refer back to chapter 8 for specific tools and techniques to help track your most important numbers.

Effectiveness ratios are a direct indication of skill level. The better the ratios, the more effective your persuasion skills, and the less work is required to generate a given amount of sales. Analyze your ratios by keeping accurate records and comparing them with colleagues or by using your own judgement. With a clear definition of the problem you can get help by talking with your sales manager, going to a seminar, or reading a book. When you clearly define the problem, answers will begin to appear all around you. As professional salespeople we should all be continually striving to increase our effectiveness. Ratio analysis will define the areas you should focus on first.

Target Markets

After trying to serve a specific market for some period of time it may become obvious that the market either doesn't want or need what you're selling. You should be open to this possibility and, if you aren't getting the response you expected, question whether you are going after the right market. But don't make this decision lightly. Changing target markets is a *strategic* decision and should be made only after all the implications have been considered. You don't want to be changing markets too often. It takes a long time to build a reputation and a network of referral sources within a given market, but in some cases changing markets is warranted.

Several years ago, I decided to enter banking as a new market for my speeches and seminars. I worked for several months calling on banks and talking with the presidents of the two major banking associations in my state. It didn't take long to realize I was getting a very cool reception. My area of expertise is communication, motivation, and effectiveness skills. At the time, banking was going through major changes trying to respond to new government regulations that were a result of the S&L failures. The banking industry had done a great deal of management and sales training in the past, but now all they could focus on was trying to comply with a barrage of new government regulations. Any training dollars they had were spent on government compliance. What I learned after several months of work was that the banking industry really didn't have need of my services, at least not in the short term. I decided to stay in touch with those people I'd met who could help me in the future, and in the short term move on to a new market.

There are times when a market you thought would be very lucrative just doesn't pan out. Don't jump to this conclusion too quickly, but as you look back at the results of your activity, consider whether the market you are targeting is responding at the level you need to meet your sales objectives.

Change Your Sales Strategy

The fifth and final area to consider when refining activity is your sales strategy. Here you want to consider whether the strategy you are using to penetrate your target market is indeed working. Sales strategies are built around specific target markets. Given a market, a strategy answers the question, "How will I go about reaching decision makers and persuading them to buy?" Strategy tells us *how* we sell, and defines the selling process. The process map in figure 11.5 is a visual illustration of a typical sales strategy.

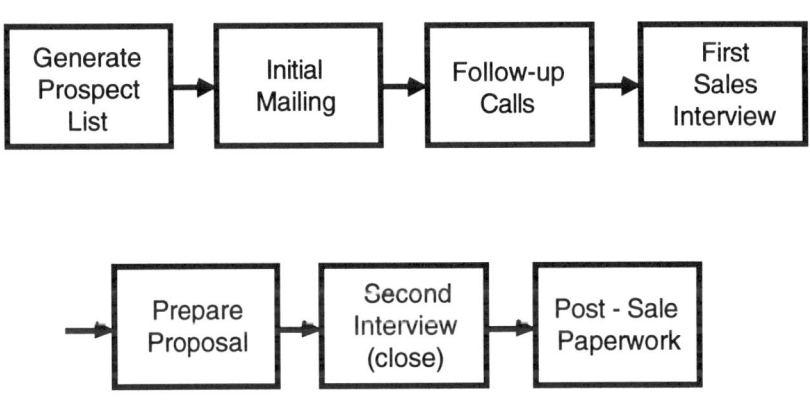

Figure 11.5: A Typical Sales Process

Refining your selling process is an exercise in process improvement. What you want to do is look at your process and ask a series of questions.

Table 11.1 Process Improvement Questions

1. Are there steps that are missing?
2. Are there steps that aren't adding value that could be deleted?
3. Where are the bottlenecks in the process? Do individual steps need to be streamlined?
4. Does the order of the steps need to be changed?

If we analyze our example in figure 11.5, and ask the question, "Are there any steps missing?" we are asking if there are things we aren't doing that might help in generating more sales. One possible answer would be to do some research and learn as much as possible about a prospect before contacting them. Obviously this would have more application for some types of businesses than for others. But the question we are asking applies to every sales process, "Are there other things I should be doing to increase the likelihood of making sales?"

The second question asks which of the steps are not adding value, which ones might be deleted. This is an important question to consider because your most precious selling resource is your time. You can't afford to waste it in unnecessary or unproductive activity. In our example, after some experience with this process, we may decide that the initial mailing really isn't adding much value. It takes a lot of time and we could just as effectively contact prospects directly by phone. We could refine our selling process by deleting the step of mailing out information before we call. This creates an immediate and significant increase in productivity. Another step that adds no value to generating sales is post-sale paperwork. This is the internal paperwork required to deliver the product or service you have just sold. Of course it is essential that the paperwork be done, but perhaps not by you. You might be able to delete it from *your* selling process by delegating it to a clerical staff person in the company or hiring an assistant to help you.

Are there individual steps that need to be improved or streamlined? Every step is a candidate for this question. If a step is causing a bottleneck and it can't be eliminated, then you have to ask how you can improve or streamline that step. A good candidate in our example would be generating a prospect list. Locating, recording, and tracking prospects is a time intensive task. When you want to streamline an individual step, it's a good idea to create a separate process map showing all the details of that step. Figure 11.6 shows a more detailed process map for the step called "Generate Prospect List."

From this more detailed process map we can now go back and ask the questions in table 11.1, "Are there missing steps? Steps that need to be deleted? Steps that need to be streamlined?" We might want to buy a Moody's index and save the trip to the library. Or per-

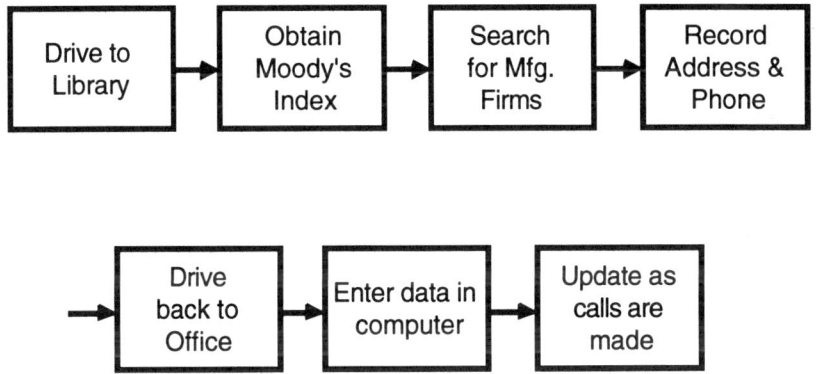

Figure 11.6: The Prospecting Process

haps buy the index on computer disk and save all the effort in entering it in the computer. In today's high tech world it is always good to consider how you can apply technology to simplify or streamline your work.

Finally, ask yourself if it would increase the effectiveness of your selling process to change the order of some of the steps. Perhaps we should mail information after we've made our initial contact by phone. Or maybe there is a way to come to the first meeting with a proposal in hand, eliminating a need for the second meeting. Consider any way that rearranging steps would increase your productivity.

Reexamination of the selling process requires questioning each of the steps you use to carry out your sales strategy. Though it's not in the nature of most salespeople to be this analytical, it is none-the-less critical if you want to optimize the effectiveness of your activity. You need to understand exactly what you are doing and why. In the past 10 years, American corporations have spent hundreds of millions of dollars training their employees to use process improvement skills. If it's that valuable for them, there must be something we can learn as well. If you haven't already, take a few minutes right now to review the information in chapter 4 so you can define your selling process and begin answering some of the questions we've posed in this section.

Activity Is Not Enough

If you want to be a top producer, it's not enough to only generate a lot of activity, you must also be forever on the lookout for opportunities to refine and improve your activity so it has maximum impact. We don't want activity for the sake of activity, we want activity that achieves results. The focus of this chapter has been to look back at the activity you've created and explore ways to make it more effective. If you can find a way to go from successfully closing one of every 20 prospects to one of every 10, you've essentially doubled your sales volume with little or no additional effort. There are an infinite number of things you could consider doing to increase the effectiveness of your activity. We've explored five in this chapter.

Conclusion
Back to Why

"If you pursue excellence through activity for the purpose of gaining inner peace, fortune will come unsought."
-- Russell Merck

In chapter 1 I made clear my belief that knowing how to create activity is only of value if you also know why. No one makes significant behavioral changes without having a clear reason for doing so. We've spent the last seven chapters learning about *how* to increase activity, and as this book draws to a close, I want to return briefly to the all important question of *why* you should work at becoming the master of your own behavior.

For anyone who makes their living in Activity-Based Selling, I have one final bit of advice: *either learn to manage your activity or get out of this profession.* At first glance you might think this rather harsh statement means that if you can't manage your behavior, you'll never make a lot of money in sales. While it's true that you *must* manage activity to excel in sales, that's not the basis for my advice. I'm more concerned about you, what happens deep inside of you, in your heart of hearts, in the deepest core of respect and liking you have for yourself. More than any other profession, Activity-Based Selling shines a light on your level of effort for you and the entire world to see. If you fail to manage your behavior, Activity-Based Selling will destroy your self-esteem and any chance you have at inner happiness.

Inner happiness is experienced as a quietness inside or a sense of wholeness and contentment. The internal struggles, strife, and frustrations we experience most of the time are replaced by a serene, relaxing calm. People who have a great deal of inner happiness enjoy themselves and the other people in their lives more than those who don't. Their peace and contentment shines through and touches others, making inwardly happy people a joy to be around. Although cars and homes and swollen bank accounts can create temporary excitement, they are not a source of inner happiness. Inner happiness is a peace and contentment generated from things inside, not outside. Inner happiness is a wonderful state we've all experienced from time to time, and it is the emotional state we seek all our lives.

I remember days in my sales career when I left the office with an empty feeling inside because I knew I had not given my best effort. These were the days when I came in a few minutes late, left a few minutes early, made lots of personal phone calls, and spent a large part of the day talking with my colleagues rather than working. I was more waiting for the day to end than aggressively pursuing my goals. While it's normal to have days like this from time to time, I was having far too many of them. And this less than stellar performance was beginning to affect how I felt about myself.

During those days I didn't have much inner happiness. My behavior was beginning to slowly erode the respect I had for myself. Having a clear set of goals to pursue and not pursuing them was tearing me up inside. And it didn't just affect me at work. I couldn't enjoy my weekends as much, or the time I spent around the house, or the time I spent with my wife, because of the inner knowledge that I wasn't doing all I was capable of. I have always connected a great deal of my self-worth to the effort I expend in pursuit of my goals. Because my effort was low, so was my self-esteem.

Having had the opportunity to speak to thousands of salespeople over the past few years, I know I'm not the only one who has experienced this. Most people compensate for this attack on their self-esteem by never being totally honest with themselves. They don't keep accurate records of what they do each day, and so in their confused and hectic lives they fool themselves into believing they are doing more than they really are. They will tell you the reason they don't keep records is because it's tedious and time consuming. But the truth is they are scared of what they might find. Though they have convinced themselves that they are giving it their all, in their heart they know the truth. And that inner knowledge blocks the peace and contentment they so desperately crave.

Others try to avoid feelings of inadequacy by distracting themselves. They try to heal the wound inside by looking for happiness outside. They spend a great deal of time and energy with their homes, cars, boats, stereos, and big screen t.v.'s to distract themselves from a deep unsettledness inside. There is nothing wrong with finding pleasure in material possessions. They can and should be a great source of pleasure ... but they are no replacement for *inner* happiness. And your enjoyment of these external pleasures will be greatly diminished if you are lacking internal pleasure.

The funny thing is, if you consider the energy and effort required to be dishonest or to distract yourself, and if you consider the negative feelings it generates, it is actually *easier* to just do the work. Next time you're supposed to pick up the phone and your mind goes into overdrive trying to figure a way out of it, save yourself some time and energy and just do it. Stop thinking about it, stop running away from it, and just do it. You'll accomplish a lot more and feel a lot better.

I will always remember the day one of my most respected mentors called me on the carpet for just doing enough to get by. He told me he knew what I was capable of, and it was a shame to see me not living up to it. I left his office that day with a new resolve to apply myself fully. In the months that followed, my activity did increase dramatically and so did my sales. But the real benefit was the way I felt every day. Gone was the strange unspoken feeling of guilt, replaced by pride and energy, and a much greater self-respect. To this day I value more highly the weeks where I fully extend myself than even the weeks when I close more sales.

All human beings are born with an inner need to achieve and create. We all want to find meaning and purpose in our lives. And it is the knowledge that we have applied our efforts and talents in pursuit of some worthy goal that brings fulfillment and inner happiness. What so many fail to realize is that it is the *aggressive pursuit* rather than the attainment of a goal that brings fulfillment.

I am making the assumption that at this point in your life, excellence in Activity-Based Selling is a worthy goal for you. Perhaps it is a worthy goal because you want to develop skills that will be used elsewhere, or because your sales job is providing the financial fuel to pursue other goals, or maybe because Activity-Based Selling is a lifetime career. Whether you plan to be in this type of sales for the next twelve months or the next 30 years, it will be your *pursuit* of excellence during that time (rather than the attainment of some goal) that will bring fulfillment. If you can learn to pursue excellence for the sake of excellence, for the way it makes you feel inside, external results will take care of themselves.

The dangers of inner strife and reduced self-esteem caused by poor job performance are much greater for an activity-based salesperson than for most people. In many jobs someone else manages your activity for you. If you're a sales clerk in a department store, how much you do is controlled by the number of customers who walk through the door. It's hard to not do your job when you have a customer standing two feet away asking for your help. In corporate jobs your boss helps manage your activity. He assigns projects, sets goals, and monitors progress. In the corporate setting your co-workers also hold you accountable to your goals because they depend on your work output to do their jobs. But as an independent, activity-based salesperson, no one manages your activity for you. You can very easily perform below your potential and no one will ever know ... *except you*. And that knowledge will destroy your inner happiness. As activity-based salespeople we *must* stay on top of our activity. For the sake of our own happiness, we must become the masters of our own behavior.

While it's true that the dangers of not managing activity are higher for activity-based salespeople, so too are the rewards if you *do* master your activity. Because activity management is really an inner exploration (managing your emotions, disciplining yourself, being totally honest with yourself), those who are willing to go through this exploration emerge much stronger, knowing themselves at a deeper level, with greatly increased confidence and self-esteem. Having this type of job is the greatest thing in the world, because if you master the job, that success overflows into the rest of your life. In the same way that not managing your activity will diminish the quality of your entire life, becoming the master of your behavior will expand it.

In the end of chapter 1 I said that if you pursue excellence through activity for the purpose of gaining peace of mind, fortune will come unsought. Throughout this book I've tried to motivate you by promising you inner peace rather than financial rewards. But let's face it, motivation doesn't have to be an either/or proposition, it can be both. We can be motivated by a desire for inner fulfillment *and* a desire for financial abundance. And if you are motivated by financial success, I have some good news for you: *you are much closer to abundant financial success than you could possibly know.*

For most of my life it seemed that I was pushing and struggling very hard just to survive. It seemed like all I could do just to pay the mortgage. When I saw people who owned businesses, had nice cars, and were members of the country club, they seemed so much different than me. Though I really wanted to be like them, that life seemed light-years away, more fantasy than possibility. I didn't see how I could ever put forth the kind of effort that level of success must require.

One of the most important realizations of my life was that those people were not significantly different from me. The effort I was putting into survival (paying my bills, maintaining my house, doing my job) was significant. No one can be managing all that without significant effort. But those other people were earning ten times what I was. How were they doing it? Were they superhuman? If I was working 40 hours a week, were they working 400? What was their secret? When I talked with these people I was surprised. They didn't seem superhuman. They were highly active, they were expending a lot of effort; but only slightly more than I was. I began to think that maybe that little extra effort was their secret, a small difference that makes all the difference.

Most people believe that success is beyond their grasp, just something to daydream about while they live out their gray, monotonous, mediocre lives. The cruel irony is that if they could just get themselves to do a little more, if they would just stretch a little further, they would experience success beyond what they only dared dream of.

> *"There is only a fine line of effort that separates mediocrity from greatness."*
>
> *-- Earl Nightingale*

I had been operating with a distorted view of reality. I thought I was only doing 5% of what it took to be successful with 95% to go. In reality I was doing 95% with only 5% to go. Think of all the effort, all the years of practice, of playing little league, high school, college, and minor league baseball that are required just to get to the major leagues. There's a tremendous amount of effort that goes into just getting to play the game. But once you get there, it is the person who puts forth the tiny little bit of extra effort - to come to practice early, to spend a few extra minutes with the hitting coach, to take a little extra batting practice - who hits .300 instead of .250. And the .300 hitter makes more money, has more fans, and does more commercials than all the .250 hitters combined. Compared to the effort required for survival, the extra effort required for success is infinitesimal ... but it makes a huge difference in the outcome. A musician invests years in learning to play his or her instrument, but it is the person who practices an extra half-hour a day who is considered a virtuoso. A winning runner finishes a race only a fraction of a second ahead of his competitors.

There *is* only a fine line of effort that separates mediocrity from greatness.

Whatever your line of work, I can assure you that the most successful are only working slightly harder than the least successful. Give a little more, stretch a little further and see what a difference it makes. A little extra effort goes a long way. That little extra effort may well be the key that unlocks financial success beyond your wildest dreams.

Can you really do it? Can you really push a little harder, work a little more, and become one of the very special people that the rest of us read about and look up to? You bet you can. I guarantee it! I can guarantee it because just from the relationship we've shared as you read this book, I know several important things about you. First, I know that you've shown great commitment in seeing this book through to the end. You've shown that you want to be better, to grow and to improve. And if you want to grow you will. Second, I've challenged you - even accused you at times - of not doing all you're capable of. Perhaps it made you uncomfortable or even angry, but you didn't put the book down and stop reading. You were open enough to consider the possibility that you could do more. And the first step to doing more is honestly admitting that you can do more. And third, I know you are a human being. Whether you know it or not, whether you believe it or not, you have an incredible capacity to achieve and create. The stories of history are bursting with examples of tremendous achievements reached by supposedly normal people. It's in all of us to do whatever we set our minds to. If you set your mind to being a master sales professional I *can* guarantee you will be successful.

A Final Word

We are now at the end of this book, and I want to take this opportunity to say thank you. Thank you for the faith you had in buying the book, for the commitment you've shown in seeing it through to the end, and for allowing me to share my ideas with you. It is my heartfelt wish that as you implement some of these techniques you will witness a significant increase in your activity and thereby your results. Most of all I hope that you experience the daily happiness and fulfillment that come from doing all you are capable of. There is no greater gift in life than to be happy from moment-to-moment. It is this happiness that I wish for you. Good luck and God bless you.

Index

A

Activity-Based Selling	2
Activity Levels, Increase	179
Activity Logs	122-127
Allen, James	163
Anxiety	103
Aristotle	167
Arousal (Emotions)	95-96
Arrival Position	82, 140

B

Beach Scene	85
Behavior	
Imaging Positive	81
Shaping	117
Belief Statements	33
Beliefs	
Definition	24
Identifying Limiting	32
Integrating Enabling	33
Blood Sugar	66
Branden, Nathaniel	79
Breathing, Power	73-74
Brick Wall Metaphor	16, 18-20
Bush, George	141
Buxton, T. F.	168

C

Caffeine	72-73
Catching Yourself	
in the Act	103
Challenges of ABS	3-4
Change Nothing	176
Choline	75
Circadian Rhythms	61
Classical Conditioning	97
Conditioned Responses	97
Conditioning Book	166
Consistency	28, 181-183
Creating Sales Activity	
Through Mental Imaging	88
Critical Mass	180-181
Csikszentmihaly, Mihaly	160

D

Data,	
Graphical Display	131-133
Debilitating Emotions,	
Identifying	102
Depression	
Definition	55
Techniques for	56
Dietary Habits	56-61
Dietary Supplements	74-75
Dimethelglycine (DMG)	75
Disappointment	103
Discipline	
Beware Overuse	151, 153
Definition	139
Developing	143
Recognizing Opportunities	145
When to Use	144
Discretionary Tasks	35, 62
Dolphin Show	117
Dumbbell Rack	148

E

Effectiveness Ratios	184-187
Emotions	
Causes of	96
Definition	95
Physical Components	95
Techniques for	105

202 • Activity-Based Selling

Energy Boosters	63-76
Environment, Managing	110
Exercise, Aerobic	64

F

Fat, Calculation of %	58
Fears about ABS	6
Feedback	161
Flow	160
Focus	161
Fruits and Vegetables	59
Frustration	102

G

Ginseng	75
Glycemic Index	67
Glycemic Response of Selected Foods	69
Goals	37-41, 161
Guilt	103
Gym Membership	66

H

Hedonic Tone	95-96
Honesty, The Need for	13

I

Implementing Techniques for Managing Emotions	112
Independence	4
Inner Happiness	13, 194
Insulin	66
Internal Dialogue,	156
Times to Use	159

J

Juicing	60

L

L-carnitine	75

LA Lakers	137
Lag Time	146, 177-179
Lemons, Fresh	87
Lethargy	102
Level, Appropriate ~ for Key Sales Activities	41

M

Mackenzie, Alec	161
Mandino, Og	163
Marine Corps	15
Meaning (as a cause of emotions)	98
Meaning, Questions for	107
Meditation	70
Mental Imaging	
Best Times to Practice	89
Time Required	90
Motivation, Definition of	7

N

NBA Finals	121
Needs, Basic	100
Nightingale, Earl	198

O

Overwhelm	102

P

Paralysis by Analysis	164
Pavlov, Ivan	97
Peabody, Mr.	108
Perception	99
Performance Indices	130
Perpetuating Behavior	119
Perspective, Get Some	110
Phone calls	83-84
Phone Log	122-127
Physical State	101
Positive Reinforcement	117

Process Goals, Types of
   Amount   39
   Length of Time   40
   Time Limit   40
Process Improvement   189
Process vs. Results Goals   37
Protein   60
Public Commitment   169

R

Ratio Analysis   184-187
Reagan, Ronald   106
Rejection   4, 103
Relaxation   68
   Response   70
   Techniques for   71
Repetitive Reading   162
Responsibility   20
Restless Sleep   53
Results Equation   2
Rhon, Jim   12
Riley, Pat   137
Robbins, Anthony   168

S

Sales Activities, Classes of   35
Sales Builders   39
Sales Process   34
Sales Strategy,
   Change Your   188-201
Senses
   Qualities of   85
   The Five   84
Sleep Deprivation   52-54
Sleep, Amount Needed   53
Snore Guard   54
Stereo, Behavior Model   83
Strategy Based Selling   3
Subconscious Knowledge   11
Sugar Blues   66

T

Target Markets   187-188
Time Frame (process goals)   41
Time Log   128
TOTE   82
Tracking
   Applied to Phone Calls   84
   Definition   117

U

Uncle Joe & Cousin Ben   16
Urges   140, 149

V

Visceral Sensations   95
Visual Reminders   164
Visualization   80, 150
Vitamins   74

W

Wheat Germ   75
Wortman, Judith   60

Y

Yield   5

About the Author

An activity based salesperson himself, Russ Merck has many years of practical experience in the art of self-motivation. As an author and speaker, he has conducted seminars for professional associations and major corporations in ten countries on three continents. If you want to learn more about Activity-Based Selling, consider having Russ deliver a speech or seminar for your company, or ask about the audio series that supplements the information in this book. For more information, write or call:

The Center for Personal Effectiveness
60 Vernon Street
Hamden, CT 06518
(203) 248-4543